# Architecture of the World

Jean-Louis de Cenival
Henri Stierlin (Ed.)

# Egypt

Photos: Henri Stierlin
Preface: Marcel Breuer

Benedikt Taschen

Editor of series    Henri Stierlin
Plans    Georges Berthoud EPF SIA

Editor of English edition    Kenneth Martin Leake

# Contents

# The Contemporary Aspect of Pharaonic Architecture

Preface by Marcel Breuer, architect

There is a quality in Pharaonic architecture that, despite our twentieth century environment and outlook, fascinates us more and more. It is of particular interest not merely to the archaeologist or the connoisseur, but also to the architect who seeks the origins of his own work.

Our technology is that of steel, reinforced concrete; theirs was the technology of stone and mud brick. Our approach is a scientific one, moving faster and faster toward new discoveries and new solutions; it changes continuously, and has altered fundamentally the image of our cities in the last seventy-five years. The approach of the Pharaonic peoples was a traditional one, holding fast for 2,500 years to variations of the same image. Our philosophy is influenced by the miracle of modern communications; theirs was based on limitation of thought and on isolation. Theirs was a society of great social differences, ruled by a concentration of absolute might. Ours is moving towards equality of classes and power controlled by society.

Our society, our beliefs, our methods, our culture seem utterly different from those of ancient Egypt. Consequently, some interrelation of their social background and ours does not offer an easy explanation of the attraction their pyramids and monoliths and temples hold for us.

To say that our relatively new admiration and curiosity for those ruins springs from a fascination with strange and mysterious things is only part of the truth. If we explore our feelings more thoroughly, we find that a good deal of specific, direct comprehension is involved. We discover we have some roots in common with those ancient builders; we find, in some important aspects, that their architecture is 'modern'. Both cultures have a similar responsibility toward the material of construction. Both tend to create characteristic, basic and unmistakable expressions of their technology; both exploit to the utmost the function and the potential form of their available material. The Great Sphinx expresses monolithic rock; the bridges of Maillard clearly say reinforced concrete. The Eiffel Tower could be of no other material than steel; the Crystal Palace could be only of glass. The pyramids could have been made only of stone blocks. The Pharaonic builder employed his material with an authority, a force and a sophistication that has never been surpassed; no one has better learned the language of gravity, of weight and of the stone cube. Nowhere else, and at no other time, has the stone mound been transformed so directly and so basically into geometry.

The concept of broad simplicity is another trend with which our contemporary aims are in sympathy. Which other period of the past had the courage to tilt a triangle seven hundred feet long against another of equal length?

Theirs was the inherent boldness and lyricism of large dimensions. Physical size as an aesthetic fulfilment in itself; no apology, no ornamental modulation; one continuous stone texture bound only by sky, rock and sand; great contrasts of surface, of form and of elemental geometry: this is the architecture of ancient Egypt.

Our contemporary work is governed by comparable instincts: the rhythm of steel cables shading a mile of air; the continuous exposed fibres of a façade with its texture of glass, metal, concrete, seven hundred feet long, seven hundred feet high. An important segment of our contemporary philosophy, although by no means the whole, shows here innate similarities to the Pharaonic one, although differently expressed in material, in form, and in social meaning.

There are other Egyptian ideas and forms that make us feel directly involved: the interrelation of open, closed and half-open spaces, for instance; ramps connecting varied levels or developing into roof terraces or into closed passage-ways; the surprise of coming from narrow approaches into bright courts; the

Church at Muskegon, Michigan, by Marcel Breuer and Herbert Beckhard (1961); maquette

Step pyramid of Zoser at Saqqara (c.2800 B.C.)

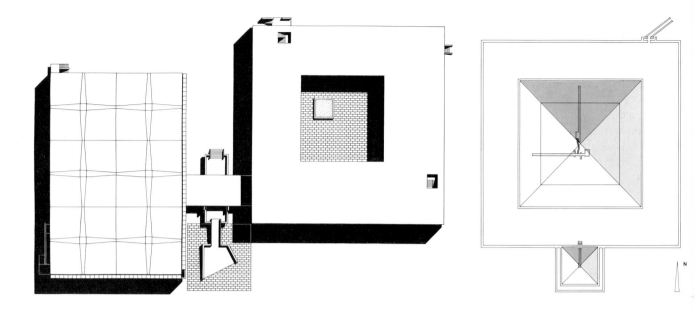

Hunter College, Bronx, N.Y., by Marcel Breuer, Robert Catje and Eduardo Catalano (1955); outline plan

Plan of the Bent Pyramid at Dahshur (c.2700 B.C.)

physical and visual experience of the third dimension as we move, mounting and descending, from space to space.

The juxtaposition of rough rock to the rectangular composition of monolithic architecture is yet another creation of the Pharaonic architects. So also is the geometrical, negative void of hewn-out space alongside great organic forms, or carved-out figures equally integrated with the architecture and the basic rock.

We are directly interested in this art of the great and simple statement, composed of elements of primitive force allied to unsurpassed sophistication of detail, with fine, sensitive bas-reliefs and hieroglyphs completely subordinated to the architecturally flat surface.

The photography presented in this book makes

us very much aware of modern aspects of Pharaonic buildings, more aware, for example, than I personally had ever been before. The discipline of the material is here visually demonstrated: the transformation of the stone pile into the pyramid takes place before our eyes.

New York
September, 1963

# Introduction

That part of Egyptian architecture which was built to last was religious in character. Secular buildings, erected for everyday use, were constructed of rough brick, mud, or wood, and, apart from some forts, mainly in Nubia, such as those recently discovered at Buhen and Mirgissa, and a few subsidiary temple buildings like the store-rooms at the Ramesseum, they have almost completely disappeared. Sometimes the ground plan, decorative fragments, the bases of walls, or stone features such as door surrounds have survived, enabling an approximate restoration to be made. In this way we have a fairly exact idea of what the palace of Amenophis III at Thebes, the palaces and villas of Amarna, and the workers' village at Deir el Medineh looked like. Nevertheless, these remains are never sufficient for an aesthetic impression to emerge from the ruins, and, as this book is not concerned with archaeology, they have no place here.

In Egypt, as in many other countries, every religious building was simultaneously utilitarian—a place of worship or a tomb—and a kind of symbol. The ancient Egyptians did not distinguish between these two functions. The symbolic power of the temple plans, the images graven on the walls, and the forms of worship, all led to the same goal; a goal, that was both spiritual, as it involved setting superhuman forces in motion, and practical, in that the final awaited result was the maintenance of the country's prosperity. Their architecture aimed to be purely functional, just as ours so often does. As Le Corbusier regards a building as a 'machine for living in', so the Egyptian temple was a machine for maintaining and developing divine energy. This more or less common goal helps us to regard Egyptian art as something vital and alive. To do this we must forego approaching it as an interplay of forms against a vague historical, archaeological or esoteric background, nor must we apply to it, either consciously or

The god Thoth, patron of hieroglyphic writing

these ancient master builders, to determine their aims and the means they had at their disposal to attain them. In short, we shall endeavor to reconstruct their creative process. Clearly, it is possible only partially to succeed in doing so. Every work of art, whether or not it be architecture, indicates its creators' attitude to the world, and to the current political, social and cultural environment. We may have an idea of the problems and of the means available to overcome them, but they were the problems and solutions of men working against a background different from ours. We cannot put ourselves in their place, even with the help of the knowledge we have collected about their civilization.

It is first and foremost necessary to have some knowledge of the historical and cultural background of Egyptian architecture, however sketchy it may be. Within the confines of this book it is not possible to recount the history of the country with its successive rulers and their wars, to study the administrative machinery, to list the countless gods, and to retail the exploits attributed to them. There are many books available which do this and the reader who wishes to gain a more exact picture of Egyptian civilization will find a concise bibliography at the end of the present volume. We must, however, begin this survey with a sketch of the basic features of this civilization and the aspects which it offered at various stages of its history. Tourists who pay quick visits to the ruins of the ancient monuments or visit the Egyptian galleries of the Louvre or the British Museum usually get the impression that Egypt looked much the same for over three thousand years. The same mysterious writing composed of birds, rabbits, flowers and weird symbols quickens the ancient stones and the temple walls, where the same gods pass by with motionless gestures and animal heads blend with their human bodies. Egypt, an unchanging land of conservative tradition, is an idea very widely held, even by

unconsciously, the criteria we are accustomed to applying to buildings prior to the twentieth century. Rather we must try to see it in relation to the basic preoccupations of the architecture of our own time—the relationship between form and function, and constructional techniques. We shall attempt to understand the spiritual, technical and aesthetic problems that beset historians. It was also shared by the ancient Egyptians who were conscious of carrying on their civilization, living according to the same traditions, worshipping the same gods, and writing the same language. It is possible that this impression of stability was based on a number of characteristics recurring at all periods of Pharaonic history, embracing every aspect of the country's life, including religion, politics, the social order, and aesthetics. It is the sum of the characteristics that allows us to define the place of Egyptian civilization in relation to other civilizations. They constitute

Hieroglyphs: Ptolemaic inscription carved in stone

its permanent structure, to use a term employed in architectural history. Certainly, in no other country after the paleolithic age, can so many constant elements be found over so long a period. This sense of permanence was made possible by exceptionally favorable geographical and historical conditions. Its importance must not be exaggerated, however; this impression of immobility is as much due to the remoteness of their civilization as to these factors. The products of a single or a collective civilization are liable to seem more uniform the further back they are in time and the more unfamiliar they are. In fact, many branches of Egyptian culture developed very rapidly and most of its products can be exactly dated by specialists. Architecture is no exception; if we wish to understand its development, we must first get a comprehensive idea of its permanent features and then grasp the differences between the successive styles. This permanent framework can be evoked only by putting together various features, and the resulting picture will vary widely according to which features we emphasize. For us, their importance will be gauged in relation to their reaction on architecture. A number of individual characteristics which have a particularly direct bearing on this branch of art will be dealt with at the end of Chapter I; they include royal theology, temple life and ritual, mathematics, and the organization of the workshops for public works. We shall here deal with the general characteristics of geography, political, administrative and social structure, religion, and ways of thought, all of which had a more indirect influence on buildings.

Egypt's geographical position to a great extent explains the permanence of its civilization: situated on the very edge of the Near East with its warrior civilizations, it was separated from it by a desert corridor which large armies found difficult to cross. This relative isolation sheltered it from the majority of the great population

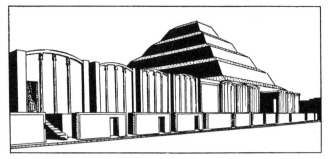

Reconstruction of the Jubilee chapels and inner court of the tomb complex of Zoser at Saqqara

movements which periodically disturbed the lives of the inhabitants of western Asia, and for more than three thousand years Egypt was able to develop practically undisturbed, slowly absorbing the influences of neighboring cultures.

The country itself, known to its inhabitants as the 'black land'—black as mud—consists of a narrow green band on the right and left banks of the Nile which has hollowed out of the desert plateau a long grooved channel bordered by cliffs which are sometimes almost perpendicular and often more than 300 feet high. Sometimes this band, squeezed between the river and the cliff, disappears altogether, and it hardly ever exceeds 12 miles in width. From Aswan which theoretically marks the southern boundary, it stretches for over 560 miles to Cairo, after which it expands into a vast delta 100 miles by 125 miles, whose total area is equivalent to that of Belgium. This zone of cultivation corresponds to the region flooded by the Nile. Swollen by the spring and summer rains which fall in the equatorial regions where it rises, the river, every year between July and October, transforms the country into a vast lake from which only the palm trees and houses emerge. Anywhere that the Nile does not reach remains desert. Left to itself, the flooded area would become a huge dried-up marsh for part of the year, and, in the delta, there are considerable

areas which have always been so. The land can be cultivated only because of the vast irrigation works involving the construction of canals and dykes and the division of the entire country into strictly defined plots bounded by small walls to hold back the water when needed, all of which requires continual watchfulness and discipline. For the ancient Egyptians to conduct this task

Valley temple of Chephren with pillars of pink granite, alabaster pavement and statues of green diorite

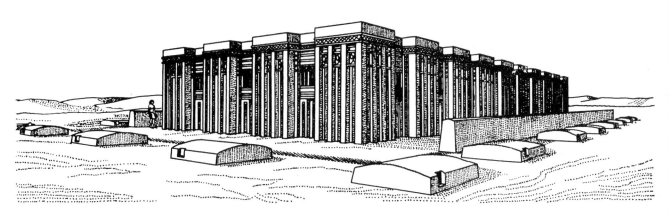

Reconstruction of a royal tomb at Saqqara dating
from the First Dynasty (3100 B.C.)

successfully, a centralized and large supply of labor, and a highly perfected administration were essential. The qualified organizers and geometricians, without whom the building of the pyramids would have been impossible, received their formative training in the school of irrigation.

These geographical features partly explain the political, administrative and social structure of the nation, which can be defined as a nation of peasants governed (through the agency of an administration that was more bureaucratic and subject to red tape than those of the modern world) by a king-god, the incarnation of the great divinities of the country, whose duty it was to assure its order and prosperity by his conduct and actions in their service. The totalitarian aspect of this form of absolute monarchy was moderated by a very strict moral concept of the part played by royalty. The Pharaoh was god, and, theoretically, the whole country belonged to him; but justice and truth were superior to him. There is no recorded example of the king intervening in a legal matter, even when it was a question of political treason, and, in normal circumstances, he probably did not have the right of life and death over his subjects to whom, in theory, he alone gave the breath of

life. We are told that King Cheops, amazed at the skill of a magician who was said to be capable of reuniting severed heads with their bodies, wished to make trial of this with a man. 'Let the prisoner who is in the prison be brought forth after his execution,' he ordered. But Djedi, the magician, replied: 'No, my sovereign master, not a human being; for it is forbidden to do such a thing to the sacred flock of God.' This concern of the Egyptians for the human person clearly distinguishes them from the majority of contemporary civilizations.

So far, we have no exact idea of the size of the population. Estimates vary from between one-and-a-half millions to over five millions. We do know, however, that it was almost exclusively composed of peasants and civil servants. Up until the Late Period there is no trace of a middle class centering round business or industry. The many towns must have been no more than groups of farms which also housed a few specialist craftsmen or laborers who worked mainly for the central power, usually represented by the temples, or for the richest civil servants and landowners. Private business, both internal and international, which developed slightly under the New Kingdom, was probably never on a large scale. Internal and international exchanges involving grain and precious metals remained in the hands of the Pharaohs. This trade still remained a form of barter even when it was based on the relative scale of the various products involved and the weights of the principal metals: gold, silver and copper. Within the framework of the great agricultural estates there existed some small private industries such as foodstuffs and textiles, but they were chiefly reserved for home consumption. The more important industries, including the manufacture of weapons, naval yards, and papyrus factories, seem to have been concentrated among the royal workshops, or in those of the temples. The country's resources continued primarily to be derived from agriculture—corn, barley, flax, oil and wine—the raising of cattle, hunting or fishing. Wild birds and fish were important features of the food supply. Thus agricultural prosperity was the highest benefit that could be granted by the gods in return for the building of their temples.

The peasants were divided among smallholdings amounting to less than $2\frac{1}{2}$ acres.

Middle Kingdom bas-relief depicting transport of a stone colossus on a sledge

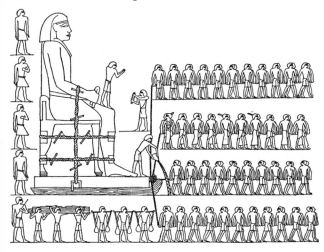

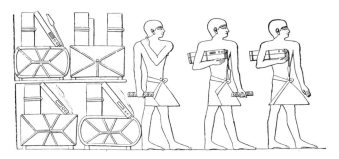

Scribes with their writing materials

These could belong to the farmer, but more often formed part of the royal estates or those of the temples or of the great landowners who were usually civil servants. Little is known of the definition and the rights of property, so words such as 'possession' and 'landowner' must be taken in a very broad sense. Owners of 25, 50 or 75 acres seem to have been considered as great landowners at all periods. Except in the Intermediary Periods, vast private estates like those that existed before the 1952 revolution, were not a feature of Pharaonic Egypt.

Above this mass of peasants was a large, thriving class of civil servants. They watched over the irrigation system, worked out and collected taxes, managed the royal property, and administered justice. They were paid in kind with precious metals, food, lands and servants, and paid no taxes themselves. Almost the only people who knew how to write, they fulfilled the most important duties of the priests; intellectual, literary and religious life developed in their society. This inflated administration was headed by one or two chief ministers known as viziers and was divided into departments more or less similar to our own ministries. These varied according to the period, but always maintained a hierarchical organization of skilled workers ranging from the minister to humble provincial scribes. Within the structure, careers were more or less open to all; there were always families who took care to keep a share of the most lucrative posts for themselves, but there were also numerous cases of very high civil servants of simple origin, at least up to the end of the New Kingdom, when the professional classes became rigidly set. The most remarkable characteristic of this administration, especially in the Old Kingdom, was its extraordinary appetite for paper-work, an appetite that has never been equaled since. Even the smallest farm holdings were the subject of minute accounts. Part of the archives of the Pharaoh Neferirkara (Fifth Dynasty) has been discovered, revealing that, in his funerary temple, a daily account, which was restated every month, was kept of incoming and outgoing produce; tables were also drawn up defining in detail the part played by each priest and, every month, an inventory was published carefully describing the state of repair of all the furniture in the temple, including pottery and chests. Every year there was a census of the nation's cattle and an analysis of the harvests.

This professional hierarchy, composed of farmers, craftsmen and scribes, formed no more than part of the framework of the social structure, nor did the distinction between men and women have any bearing on the matter. In principle they were on an equal footing; women could own land, conduct business and testify in courts of law. All men, however, were not equal, though, theoretically, there was no distinction between them in the eyes of the gods and the law. There were no slaves in the Greek or Roman sense of the word indicating a class deprived of all civic rights, at the mercy of a master exercising the power of life or death. In Egypt the

Survey of part of the great temple at Edfu, typical of those published in the 'Description of Egypt' by the archaeologists accompanying Bonaparte's expedition

Sacrifice before a funerary chapel

term 'slave' was applied to male or female servants who could be bought, sold, or inherited, or to farmers who were attached to land that they could not abandon and could be included in its sale. These slaves were often prisoners of war or farmers who had incurred debts, but they had the right to own possessions, to buy their freedom, to marry free citizens, and to testify at law just like anyone else; the penal code seems to have made no distinctions, though our knowledge on this point is very limited. Freemen were grouped in a more subtle, less formal hierarchy, resembling the Roman system of patron and client. Influential people took under their wing, or sometimes maintained, a circle of professional subordinates, local craftsmen, and servants. This patronage continued after the benefactor's death by bequests of land which involved the obligation of providing the dead man with a portion of their products by placing them on the offertory table in his tomb. These funerary deeds of gift helped, more than anything else, to prevent the development of great estates, ensuring stability to a comfortably-endowed class of middle-sized landowners.

Quite clearly, it was their religious ideas, their certainty that the destiny of their country and culture depended on the good will and power of superhuman beings and that some form of survival was possible for them after death, that drove all of them to the construction of temples and tombs. Nevertheless, this building of great stone temples, pyramids and royal tombs was a collective matter, the responsibility for which devolved on a king. In this respect, there was no connection between private individuals and the gods.

An intimate relationship between god and man developed throughout Egyptian history, probably reaching its height during the Ramesside Period. There are many proofs, dating from this time, of individual responsibility for sin and repentance before the gods, and of the use of prayer to summon their help. There are also indications of the habitual use of magic, even in the most civilized circles, as a help to

Pharaoh offering a sacrifice

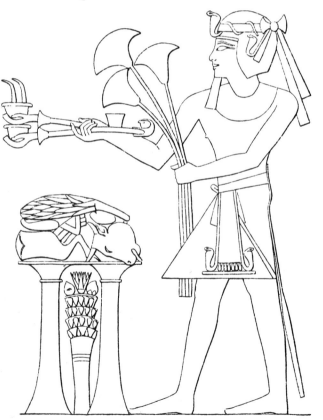

14

recovery from illness or a defence against the powers of evil, snakes, or spiteful colleagues. This sense of piety was revealed in private houses, small local sanctuaries and, sometimes, in certain parts of the temples—in front of the colossal royal statues framing the entrance, before the representations of the gods in the shrine, or in the first courtyard on the days when the god's statue emerged in procession—but it had little influence on the architecture which was determined by the national form of worship and by official theology. The god who was honored in these buildings was not the savior of private individuals, but the creator and ruler of the world, who vouchsafed prosperity to the land and life to the king. This official theology was a very complex matter, springing from the fusion of tribal religions and the beliefs of those who had come to settle by the banks of the Nile. As political unity was gradually achieved, these religions coalesced to form one which embraced all pantheons, all cosmogonies and a mingling of all contradictory legends, thriving on a single concept of the divinity, a single concept of the relationship of men and gods, and a single concept of the principal act of religion: the form of worship. This parallel evolution of politics and religion was quite in keeping with a people for whom the power of a human group and that of the gods they worshipped formed a unity. Henceforward, the connection between two groups did no more than reproduce that between their gods: there was no reason to scorn the protection of a conqueror's gods as they had shown that their power was stronger. Thus, bonds of relationship or mythology were created between gods previously unknown to one another. The structure of philosophy and the mode of thought maintained by the Egyptians until the end of the Pharaonic period also favored such a synthesis. As in all so-called primitive civilizations, philosophy was scarcely distinguishable from theology. It was composed of an accumulation of mytho-

Pharaoh making a sacrifice at the Djed pillar

logical images, some borrowed from different traditions, some contradictory, the essential point being that each shed light on one of the aspects of the mystery. Examples of this may be found in the various cosmogonies elaborated in the main centers of Egyptian religious thought. None of these sprang from an act of pure creation, or from a god existing throughout eternity in an established form, but from the original chaos within which a force takes on consciousness and shape to unleash the creative process, setting the universe in order. At Hermopolis, this primary chaos was formed by four pairs of gods and goddesses or genies whose names may best be rendered as primordial matter, the infinite, obscurity, and mystery. Transposed into our way of thinking, this means that, faced with a concept as difficult to grasp as disorganized matter or non-being, they analyzed it rationally, separating it into concepts less difficult to comprehend as they were incorporated in mythological beings. At Memphis, the god Ptah, the creative power, was separated in this way into eight gods representing both primordial matter and the creative forces employed: the heart of the god which signified his understanding and his will, and his tongue which signified his word. Other legends are based less on philosophy and more on the observation of nature and daily life. Some make the sun appear on a hill emerging from the primordial ocean, on a lotus flower, or from an egg formed in chaos. Others represent the sky as a goddess, a woman or a cow concealing the earth, absorbing the sun and offering it to the world; or as a river which the sun can traverse in his boat in the guise of a falcon or the eye of a celestial falcon. All these traditions were equally acceptable as they all made the fearful mysteries of the beyond more familiar. Each city evolved a large pantheon combining the ancient local gods with others introduced by war, alliance, commercial exchanges, or theological meditations, and sometimes confusing them. Some were the individual property of one city, others reoccurred in countless sanctuaries scattered throughout the country. All were linked by family connections which might vary from one city or period to another. This tendency to syncretism, this method of considering diverse images as aspects of the same problems ended by changing their faith in a multiplicity of gods into something very close to monotheism; each god became one of the forms or aspects of another god, one of his attributes. This view is clearly expressed in texts mainly dating from the Ramesside Period or later, although, elsewhere, they make regular references to a large number of divinities considered as individual personalities. Thus, it is difficult to speak of monotheism, except with regard to the revolution of Tell el Amarna. It was an idea that never consciously recommended itself to the Egyptians, but they did consider each of the chief gods to be unique, the primordial creator from whom everything took its source and of whom all the other gods were no more than semblances.

Every temple was built to honor one of these gods and, in it, he was the creator, capable of ensuring the permanence of the cosmic order and the prosperity of the nation, provided he received a suitable form of worship. He was aided in his task by a group of gods subordinate to him, although in other cities their parts might well be reversed.

Ptolemaic bas-relief depicting a Pharaoh about to erect a pair of obelisks in the presence of Horus (Edfu)

# Plates

## Complex of Zoser at Saqqara

21-24 **The boundary wall.** Height: 33 feet. Its bastions and alternate projections and re-entrants reproduce the decoration of a boundary or outer wall of brick or wood. This design was abandoned in later buildings but continued in use in the other arts; it may be seen on a sarcophagus (plate 23) dating from the Old Kingdom and in the vault of Unas (plate 44).

5 **The step pyramid.** This is the earliest of the pyramids, an enormous mass rising in six steps, with an almost flat top. Original height: 200 feet; base: 358 feet from north to south, 397 feet from east to west. It was built in several stages, the first of which resulted in no more than a flattened mass without steps, the constructional materials being laid in horizontal courses. This core was later covered by the present stepped erection made of blocks set at right angles to the faces. In the foreground, the remains of **Temple T.**

26 End of the **entrance colonnade.** The ceiling was carried on a series of wall-supports.

27 **The Cobra Wall:** eastern face of a building forming part of the south tomb.

28 a) **The House of the South.** Engaged column of the façade with chiselings imitating a tree-trunk.
b) Ceiling of the small inner room made of slabs set edgeways and rounded to represent wooden logs.
c) Entrance to one of the small **chapels of the jubilee courtyard.** Detail of the sham door: the lower hinge and the socket in which it was supposed to pivot.

29 Engaged columns in the form of papyrus stalks on the east side of the **House of the North.**

## The Pyramids of Sneferu at Dahshur

30 In the background, the **North Pyramid.** Center, the **South** or **Bent Pyramid.** In the foreground, the small satellite pyramid.

31 North-west corner of the Bent Pyramid.

## Tomb complexes at Giza

32 **Pyramid of Cheops.** The thin facing of fine limestone has completely disappeared.

33 Interior views of the Pyramid. a) and b) The great sloping gallery leading to the upper vault. Height: 28 feet; width: 8 feet; length: 153 feet. c) Corridor leading to the intermediary vault—the Pyramid contains three. Height $5\frac{3}{4}$ feet.

34 The **Pyramid** of Cheops and, right, that of **Chephren.**

35 **The Sphinx of Chephren.** The extremities of the paws are reconstructions. The stele in front of the creature's breast is of later date (c.1420).

36 General view of the south-east sector of the site. Left background, the Pyramid of Mycerinus. Right, the Pyramid of Chephren. Left foreground, the end of the Lower Temple of Chephren. Right, in front of the Sphinx, the remains of the temple probably built at the same period.

37 **Lower Temple of Chephren.** Rear hall. Pillars and architrave are formed of single blocks of pink granite. The floor is paved with alabaster.

38 Passage rising towards the approach road.

39 Detail of the masonry.

## Private tombs (Mastaba)

40 **Tomb of Mereruka** (Saqqara c.2320). Main chapel. The top part of the walls is a reconstruction.

41 Mereruka taking part in games and dances.

42 Statue of the dead man in a niche above his table of offerings.

43 **Tomb of Ptahhotep** (Saqqara c.2380). Poultry belonging to the dead man: geese, a swan, ducks, pigeons and little birds.

## Vault of the Pyramid of Unas at Saqqara

44 The pyramid texts are carved on the upper part of the back wall. In the foreground, the top of the royal sarcophagus.

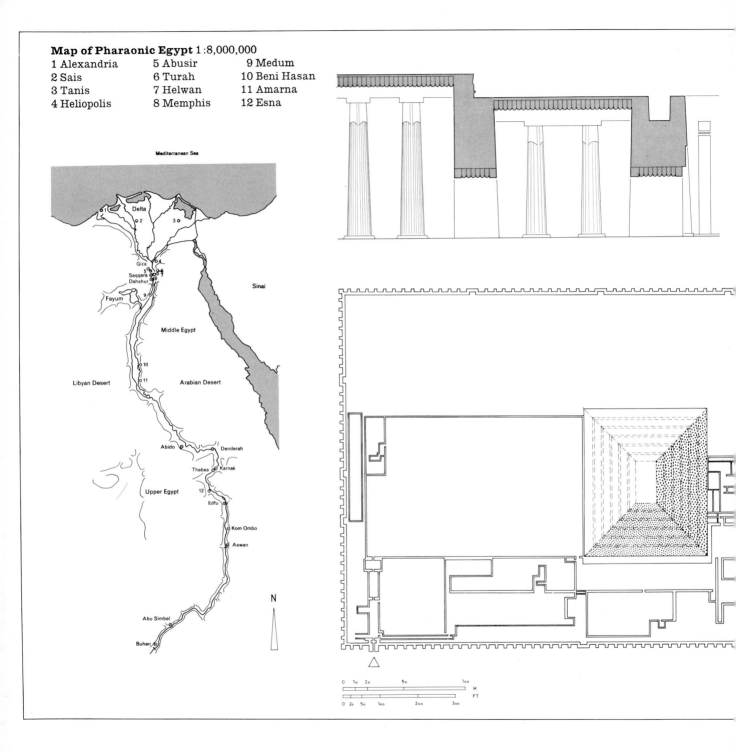

**Map of Pharaonic Egypt** 1 : 8,000,000

1 Alexandria
2 Sais
3 Tanis
4 Heliopolis
5 Abusir
6 Turah
7 Helwan
8 Memphis
9 Medum
10 Beni Hasan
11 Amarna
12 Esna

Mediterranean Sea

Delta

Giza
Saqqara
Dahshur
Fayum

Sinai

Middle Egypt

Libyan Desert

Arabian Desert

Abido
Denderah
Thebes
Karnak

Upper Egypt

Edfu

Kom Ombo

Aswan

Abu Simbel

Buhen

N

0  1o  2o        5o              1oo
                                    M
                                    FT
0  2o  5o   1oo      2oo        3oo

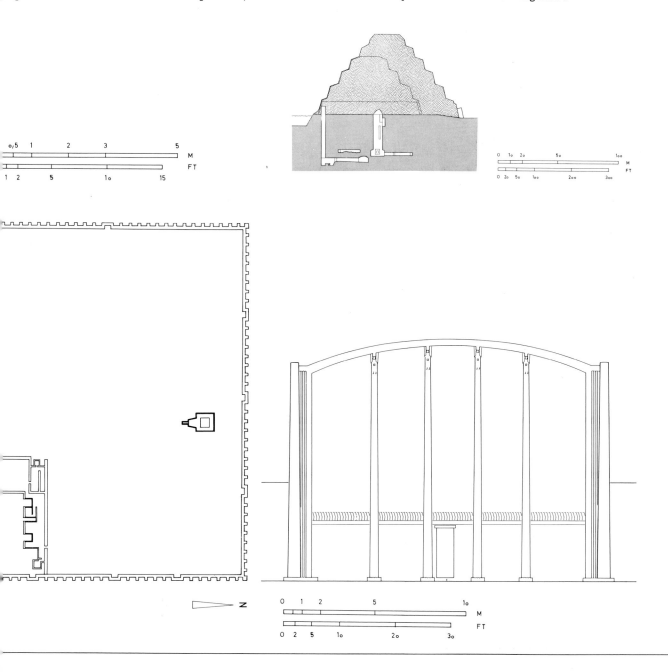

# Notes

## Tomb complex of Zoser

Third Dynasty (c.2675). This is the oldest of the pyramids and was built for King Zoser by his chancellor Imhotep on the plateau of Saqqara. It is surrounded by a group of buildings far more complex than those associated with the royal burial places and stands almost in the center of a rectangular space, 607 by 304 yards, bounded by a stone wall. The southern face of this wall supports a long, massive structure held to be the tomb of the king who was buried here in the guise of ruler of Upper and Lower Egypt. A vast courtyard stretches between this building and the pyramid. The eastern part of the enclosure is occupied by the great entrance colonnade and three court-yards, the first of which is bordered by two ranges of small chapels and is supposed to reproduce the setting of the royal jubilee. The other two courtyards are dominated by two large buildings, originally with concave roofs, called the 'House of the North' and the 'House of the South': these possibly represent the administrative centers of the two halves of the country. Against the north face of the pyramid lies another large building identified as being either the center of the royal cult or a reproduction of the royal palace. A large portion of the remaining area is taken up with long ranges of sham granaries and warehouses. This is the first complex in which stone was used as a basic material. With a few exceptions the buildings are sham and their lines reproduce those of earlier construc-tions fashioned of brick, clay and timber; inside, they are either solid or else hollowed out to form one or two small rooms. The chief ones have been partially restored by J.-P. Lauer; he was very strict in his methods and, for the most part, made use of the ancient stones. The modern features are easily distinguishable.

## The two Pyramids of Sneferu at Dahshur

Fourth Dynasty (c.2625). Two of the three pyramids built by Sneferu are at Dahshur. That known as the North Pyramid is the earliest example of the tapering, classic form. Height: 344 feet; sides of the base: about 728 feet; slope of the face: 43°.

The other is known as the South or Bent Pyramid. The latter name derives from the clear break in the slope about half way up; the lower section of each face is inclined at an angle of about 54°, the upper section at an angle of 43°. Height: 318 feet; base: 618 feet.

## Tomb complexes at Giza

Fourth Dynasty (c.2600-2500). Cheops, Chephren and Mycerinus had their tombs built on the plateau of Giza. Each complex comprised a pyramid sheltering the royal vault, a funerary temple (also known as the upper temple) attached to the eastern face of the pyramid, and a reception, or lower temple at the foot of the plateau; the two temples were linked by a long passage.

The Pyramid of Cheops was the highest ever built by the Egyptians. Original height: 480 feet; base: 755 feet; slope 51° 56'. The upper temple has been destroyed and the site of the lower temple has not been excavated.

Pyramid of Chephren. Height: 470 feet; base: 706 feet; slope: 52°, 20'. The upper temple is in a ruinous state, but the lower temple is the best preserved of all those of the Old Kingdom. It has lost its roof and its outer granite facing, but inside walls and supports are more or less intact up to ceiling level. At the side of this temple a huge sphinx, 187 feet long and 66 feet high, has been carved in the rock of the plateau here used as a quarry

Pyramid of Mycerinus. Height: 203 feet; base: 355 feet; slope: 51°. The upper temple is again in a ruinous state; the lower temple, built of brick, has been destroyed.

## The Mastabas

This name was given to the tombs built around the royal pyramids by the nobles of the Old Kingdom. They are massive rectangular structures with gently sloping walls and were originally hollowed out with niches or small chapels. In the course of the Fifth Dynasty, these chapels developed into proper rooms with pillared halls, court-yards, storehouses and so on. On their walls are carved numerous scenes of funerary cults and everyday life.

## Pyramid of Unas

Fifth Dynasty (c.2350). At Saqqara. One of the smallest pyramids of the Old Kingdom. Height: 62 feet; base: 216 feet. In the interior rooms is the oldest version of the pyramid texts.

## Bent pyramid of Dahshur
Site with lower temple 1:10,000, plan and sections 1:3,000

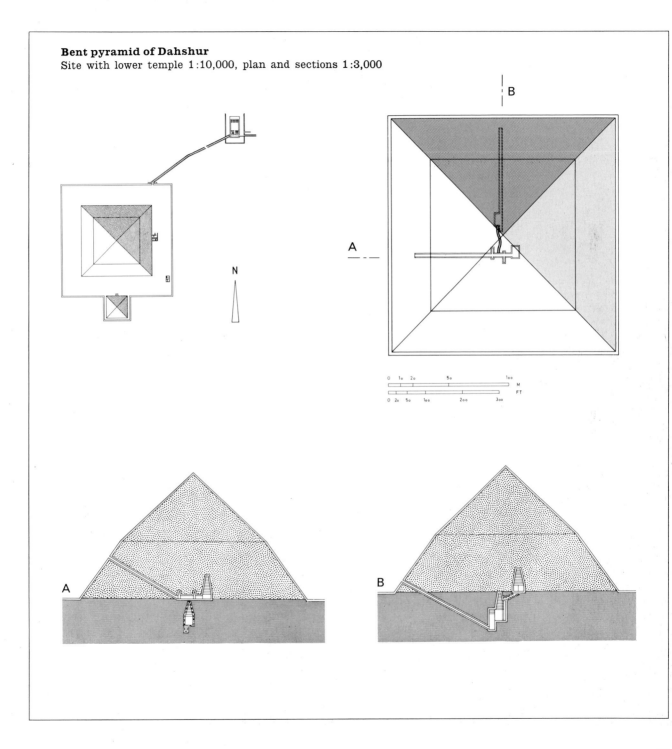

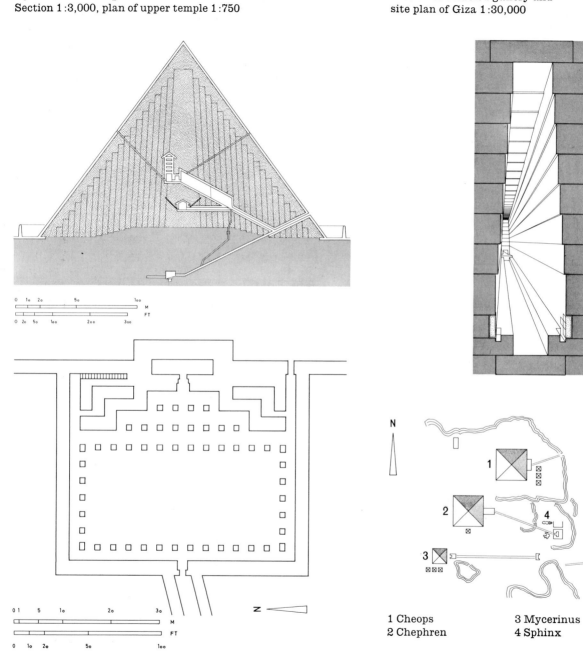

**Pyramid of Cheops at Giza**
Section 1:3,000, plan of upper temple 1:750

Section of corbeled gallery and
site plan of Giza 1:30,000

0  1o  2o  5o  1oo
M
FT
0  2o  5o  1oo  2oo  3oo

0 1  5  1o  2o  3o
M
FT
0  1o  2o  5o  1oo

N

1 Cheops
2 Chephren
3 Mycerinus
4 Sphinx

# 1. Main Stages of History and Civilization

The historical background to the development of Egyptian civilization is relatively simple. The ancients divided it into thirty-one dynasties which subsequent historians have grouped into great periods or kingdoms each presenting a more or less continuous development apparently free from serious or prolonged disturbances and possessing individual characteristics. Thus specialists can usually assign statues and stelae to specific periods without hesitation. Between the periods of these kingdoms were so-called 'intermediary' periods of disorder. Egyptian prosperity was unstable, dependent on the maintenance of irrigation channels and threatened by the nomadic shepherds from the surrounding deserts who, in the dry season, purchased grazing rights for their flocks in the Nile valley. After a few years of misrule with corn stocks depleted and dykes in disrepair, famine and disorder could ensue; the nomads would descend on the country, pillage and take possession of it.

## The formative period (c.3100-2650)

The prehistoric period came to an end round about 3100—certainly by 2850. This date is defined by two important events, the invention of writing and the unification of the country. After unification there followed a succession of three or four centuries sometimes known as the Thinite Period—from Thinis, the capital at that time—which included the first two dynasties. The essential characteristics of Egyptian civilization were soon formed, although there is insufficient information to enable historians to follow its progress step by step. We have to be content with an approximate list of rulers and a few more or less incomprehensible inscriptions recording victories over neighboring peoples, religious festivals, titles of officials and so on. Countless tombs, both of royal and private personages, afford evidence of everyday life and art.

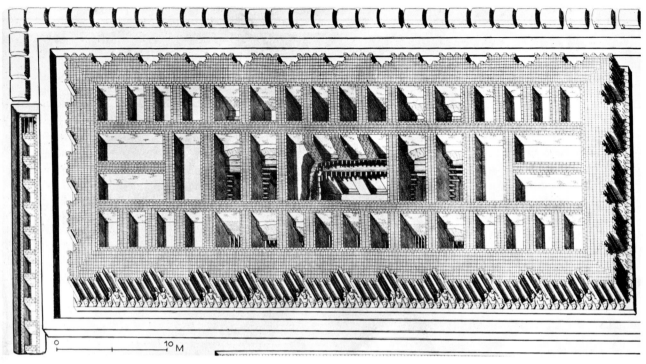

Large brick tomb of the Thinite period (reconstruction by Emery)

The largest tombs, the majority of which were royal, were formed of vast blocks of brick pierced by countless small rooms sheltering the possessions of the dead. Their decorative, recessed arcades have much in common with contemporary Mesopotamian architecture. Gradually stone came to be more often used for flooring, ceilings, door surrounds and interior buttresses.

From a political point of view less is known about the Third Dynasty, often included in the Old Kingdom, than about its two predecessors. It is dominated by King Zoser and his minister, Imhotep, builders of the Step Pyramid at Saqqara. It was in their time that Egyptian culture acquired its well-defined characteristics and great stone buildings. This period, too, saw the birth of literature and the science of medicine; it was Imhotep who wrote the first proverbs and the first medical treatise. The few contemporary inscriptions are the first that can be read, not merely interpreted.

## The Old Kingdom (c.2650-2160)

After the ferment of the preceding centuries, the Old Kingdom, by comparison, was a period of balance. This self-assured society, its politics, religion and morality ordered by the gods and ancestral example, slowly created an art of living whose rules were enshrined in wise sayings on the most mundane as well as the most profound subjects. As an example of the mundane, Kagemni advises: 'If you sit in company, spurn the bread that you like; restraint is nothing, and gluttony a vice that is easily pointed out,' and of the profound, Ptahotep says, 'Do not be proud of your knowledge, consult the ignorant as well as the learned . . . A wise word is as well hidden as a precious stone, but it can be found with the serving maid leaning over the grindstone.' Regardless of the value of such discourses, in the course of four or five centuries society developed swiftly. The three dynasties (IV—VI) of the Old Kingdom can be distinguished individually.

The Fourth Dynasty was that of the great pyramids of Sneferu, Cheops, Chephren and Mycerinus, kings whose fame is equaled only by Ramesses II. But apart from their pyramids and statues, they are virtually unknown to us— we know more of some of their subjects than of them. We gain a fairly precise idea of the administrators and society from the reliefs depicting the actions of contemporary life carved on the walls of the tombs surrounding the pyramids. They give the impression of a patriarchal government with all the important posts entrusted to members of the royal family.

During the Fifth Dynasty the royal monuments were still pyramids, but of smaller proportions. Simultaneously the princes lost their absolute leadership which passed to an intellectual hierarchy of specialized officials. With the Sixth Dynasty, the administrative and social systems slowly crumbled. The aristocratic governing class gave way to a hereditary nobility of courtiers and provincial notables devoid of specialist capabilities. The government became decentralized and lost its authority.

## The First Intermediate Period

In a ruined, pillaged land, divided into warring principalities, art was a luxury which almost disappeared. The importance of this period is based on the fact that it was the cradle of an intellectual revolution—traces of which were to remain throughout the remaining course of the history of the Pharaohs and which is preserved for us in a series of writings that count among the masterpieces of Egyptian literature. A reinvestigation of the significance of existence before and after death and of the values that justify it found its clearest and finest expression in the 'Dialogue between a man and his soul'; doubt as to what will follow death is confronted with despair in the face of what precedes it:

'We have made buildings of granite, we have erected magnificent porticoes and pyramids of perfect workmanship. Their owners became gods, but their tables of offerings are empty as the mouths of those who died on the dyke without descendants, some carried away by the flood, some by the heat . . .

'Today death stands before me like the cure for an illness, like a walk after suffering. Today death stands before me like the perfume of myrrh, like repose beneath a sail on a day of high wind . . . Today death stands before me like the desire of seeing home again after long years passed in captivity . . . '

Some time, possibly at the beginning of the Middle Kingdom, the country underwent a real social revolution accompanied by the sack of the centers of government. In the course of these years former royal privileges were completely usurped, and the Pyramid Texts which used to help the Pharaoh on his last voyage, were adapted for the use of the common dead.

## The Middle Kingdom (c.2100-1780)

After the upheavals of the First Intermediate Period, Egypt was reunified by King Mentuhotep and regained stability and prosperity. Outwardly life began again as under the Old Kingdom. Kings Amenemhat and Sesostris I,

II and III built pyramids whose temples were designed to the same plan as those of their ancestors of the Fifth and Sixth Dynasties, the court notables affected the same titles, and art rediscovered perfection. Social and spiritual revolutions are not, however, lightly abolished by royal decree. Buried beneath the old titles was an administrative structure deriving from that of the personal establishment of the princes of the First Intermediate Period. Moreover, a vast middle class composed of petty officials and craftsmen sprang up between the court and provincial aristocracies. The pattern of intellectual life however did not correspond to that of the period of the great pyramids. The Middle Kingdom was the golden age of literature. For the remainder of Egyptian history its best and least daring works were to serve as a basis for teaching and were to be copied (with many spelling mistakes) by countless scholars.

The new literature inherited the Old Kingdom's taste for proverbs, while the First Intermediate Period endowed it with lyricism, a sense of disquiet, and a quest for novelty.

It was no longer the sole aim of literature to instruct and cause reflection, it also sought to entertain with ballads and marvelous tales such as the 'Ballad of Sinuhe' and the 'Shipwrecked Sailor', to intervene in politics as in the 'Prophesy of Nefertiti', to inspire vocations as in the 'Satire of the trades' and to proclaim the fame of gods and kings as in the 'Hymn to the Nile' and 'Hymn to Sesostris III'.

## The Second Intermediate Period (Thirteenth to Seventeenth Dynasties)

As the result of a series of unknown events, Egypt again fell rapidly into decline a few years after the two most glorious reigns of the Middle Kingdom, those of Sesostris III and Amenemhat III. Ever larger groups of nomads, borne mainly from the north on the first wave of the Indo-European invasion that penetrated to the Near East, infiltrated into the ill-administered and badly-defended country where they soon settled down as masters. The northern half of Egypt was governed by foreign rulers, the Hyksos, who adopted the protocol of the former kings and maintained as their vassals the Egyptian princes of the south. From this obscure period date several mathematical, medical and literary papyri, almost all copies of earlier works. As little is known of intellectual life as of political events.

## The New Kingdom (Eighteenth to Twentieth Dynasties)

About 1580, the Egyptian princes of Thebes succeeded in routing the Hyksos and reuniting the country, thus opening the most glorious period of Egyptian history. Once again everything began anew. The Pharaohs consciously revived the traditions of the early Twelfth Dynasty, and art regained the severe perfection it had possessed in the time of Sesostris I.

For close on five centuries the country, enriched by victorious wars, was to enjoy a period of prosperity and building activity unique in its history. Numerous stone temples were built, many of which are still relatively well preserved. For the first time it is possible to follow the evolution of architecture, if not reign by reign, at least century by century. This is the period best represented in this book and includes the chapel of Amenhotep I, the temples of Deir el Bahari and Abydos, the Ramesseum, and the temples of Abu Simbel and Medinet Habu.

## The Eighteenth Dynasty (c.1580-1315)

Egypt was delivered from the Hyksos by Ahmose, Prince of Thebes. Under his leadership there began a series of victorious military campaigns which resulted in the conquest of an empire extending northwards across the whole of Palestine and part of Syria as far as the Euphrates and Orontes, and southwards along the Nile to the Fourth Cataract about 600 miles from Aswan. All the kings of the dynasty up to Tuthmosis IV played some part in this. Military operations were suspended during the twenty-two-year reign of Queen Hatshepsut, wife and half-sister of Tuthmosis II, who was appointed regent during the minority of Tuthmosis III. In fact she proclaimed herself king and reigned in his stead. She can be seen in the reliefs of her funerary temple at Deir el Bahari, dressed as a king and not as a woman, fulfilling the rites before her ancestral gods.

After her death, Tuthmosis III, sought to eradicate remembrances of her and banished her name from all monuments. He resumed the military policy of his ancestors and became a great strategist. During the reign of his successor, Amenhotep III, a complete cultural change began to come into being, which, in the religious sphere, from the time of the king's death, amounted to a revolution. Amenhotep IV (Akhenaten) carried to its extreme limits a theological doctrine of very ancient origin. He appointed himself high priest of a faith which saw in the sun, represented as a disc productive of life and light, the only divine power which the Egyptians could worship and, possibly, the sole existing divinity. The names of most of the other gods suffered the same fate as Queen Hatshepsut's at the hands of Tuthmosis III. The court left Thebes, the city of Amon, and took up residence in the new town of Amarna.

In almost every sphere, an attempt was made to ignore the old conventions and to take nature as a guide. Sculpture became expressionistic, and architectural forms which were a more direct evocation of nature were preferred to those based on geometry. This period lasted only twenty years or so. The "new" town of Amarna

was abandoned in the time of the young Tut-ankh-amon, the name of Akhenaten was obliterated, and the old gods recovered their temples and their worshippers. Everything began again as before.

## Nineteenth and Twentieth Dynasties (c.1315-1085)

Under the leadership first of Sety I and then of Ramesses II, the Egyptian armies again marched to Palestine and Syria to consolidate the enfeebled empire which was now threatened by the Hittites, a more powerful enemy than Tuthmosis III had confronted. The climax of this period was the long reign of Ramesses II which lasted sixty-seven years. This king indulged a particular taste for building. On the walls of Luxor and Karnak are inscribed his boasts of having himself taken charge of the building operations. Shortly after his death the country was assailed by Indo-European tribes who invaded the whole of the Near East and Libya but then fell into disunity and confusion. Ramesses III (1198-1166) successfully warded off the danger and helped Egypt to regain part of its glory and its empire. In the following period, in the reigns of Ramesses IV to XI, there is documentary evidence that Egypt suffered from severe economic difficulties, including inflation and famine, and political setbacks such as the sack of the tombs in the Valley of the Kings, riots, and administrative and judicial scandals.

The subjects of the kings of the Old Kingdom already included the inhabitants of Nubia beyond the present frontier of the Sudan, and during the Middle Kingdom Egyptian domination stretched well beyond it. Countless foreigners, including a large proportion of Asiatics, settled on the banks of the Nile as craftsmen or slaves, and the military expeditions of Sesostris III penetrated as far as Syria. The victories of this period brought an influx of wealth which transformed the condition of the upper classes. Short campaigns resulted in the capture or recapture of rich Syrian cities together with some of their inhabitants and herds, and the imposition of an annual tribute payable by towns which sought the protection of Egypt against their enemies. This wealth poured into the royal treasury and into officials' pockets. The large numbers of Middle Kingdom petits bourgeois were replaced by a smaller aristocracy of soldiers and technicians, which developed a more luxurious, worldly and elegant way of life than had hitherto been known in Egypt. The chief beneficiaries of these victories, however, were the gods who had given the Pharaoh the power to conquer. Indeed, the chief feature of the New Kingdom was the economic growth of the temples. Gifts of land increased along with the buildings. Little is known concerning the territorial wealth of the temples in earlier periods but it was certainly little compared to what it was under Ramesses III. Then the Temple of Amon at Thebes owned 600,000 acres and that of Ra at Heliopolis, about 110,000 acres. Though this wealth was formidable, the temples were not the real owners of it; their economic independence was strictly limited and they were considered as organisms of the state. The direction of their granaries and herds was entrusted to the king's officers, and the temples themselves paid taxes. As long as the central power was strong, its control over the property of the temples was complete.

It is easy to point out the characteristics of architecture, sculpture and fashion during the Eighteenth Dynasty by making comparisons with the Ramesside period, but it is more difficult to do the same with regard to intellectual life. Of all the relatively well preserved literary texts of the New Kingdom none can be attributed with certainty to the Eighteenth Dynasty. This society of prosperous, learned scribes for whom 'a book is better than a painted stele or a wall covered with inscriptions', took pleasure in the texts of the Middle Kingdom. They continued the ancient tradition of proverbs and scholarly and satirical literature, but abandoned the vein of pessimism except as an incitement to profit from good fortune. They liked mythological ballads, whether they were merely entertaining or full of theological reflections, and animal fables. They created the epic war poem and also produced masterpieces of love poetry which had hitherto been ill represented.

The crises of the late Twentieth Dynasty left Egypt reduced to its original territory, impoverished, demoralized and divided. In the southern half of the country the high priests of Amon were the sole possessors of power during the Twenty-

Illustration on papyrus of fables involving animals

First Dynasty. Following a temporary reunification under the leadership of former generals of Libyan origin—since the Twentieth Dynasty the army had been mainly composed of foreign mercenaries, the majority of whom came from Libya—Egypt relapsed into an almost feudal decadence (Dynasty XXII—XXIV), only to be conquered first by the kings of Nubia (Dynasty XXV), who ruled the country imperfectly for a century, and then by the Assyrians who sacked Memphis, Thebes and other cities. Only a few small monuments survive from this disturbed period which is sometimes known as the Third Intermediate Period. Of its literature and science we know nothing. On the other hand, these four troubled centuries have left us with some fine sculptures which, along with the survivals of contemporary architecture, indicate a break with Ramesside traditions and a revival of those of the Eighteenth Dynasty and the Middle Kingdom. They also indicate a rapid social development heralding the pattern of the Late Period when the population was strictly divided into professional classes, with the priests in independent isolation.

## The Late Period

Twenty-sixth or Saite Dynasty. King Psamtik I (664-610) dispersed the Assyrian invaders and reunited the country. For close on a century, his successors, Necho, Psamtik II, Apries and Amasis, ruled a country once more prosperous and capable of playing an important part on the international stage. They welcomed the first Greek mercenaries into their army and a Greek city was founded in the Delta. No important temple of the period survives. From the cultural point of view, the period was dominated by a desire to revive the country's most ancient traditions. This revival played an important part in the formation of the intellectual life of the priests in the Ptolemaic Period.

The last king of the Saite Dynasty was routed by the victorious armies of Cambyses, and, for 120 years, Egypt remained a province of the vast Persian Empire (Dynasty XXVII, 525-404), before winning back its independence and part of its prosperity for a period of sixty years (Dynasties XXVIII—XXX, 404-341). In the reigns of Nectanebo I and II there was considerable architectural activity. Although no temple has survived in its entirety, we can still see standing many features incorporated in temples of other periods. These already reveal proportions, types of columns and decorative and sculptural styles characteristic of Graeco-Roman Egypt. Indeed, the essential Ptolemaic style came into being with the arrival of Alexander.

## Ptolemaic Period

On Alexander's death his empire was divided among his lieutenants; Ptolemy I, son of Lagus, received Egypt. His successors occupied the throne until the year 30 B.C., residing in Alexandria which they made into the most important city and chief center of learning of the Hellenistic world. They adopted the protocol of the Pharaohs and, like the Roman Emperors after them, are represented on temple walls worshipping Egyptian divinities.

After the Ptolemies Egypt became a Roman province. Their fall was, however, of little significance to the inhabitants of the Nile Valley; the country was better administered and the land better irrigated, but taxes were even more crippling. The Romans wanted corn and Egypt was the chief producer in the Mediterranean world. Until the arrival of Christianity the old civilization was still quite alive, at any rate in the temples. It finally died in the course of the fourth century A.D.

From the economic viewpoint the first three Ptolemies introduced great improvements along with new cultures, better irrigation and a harvest every six months. Such innovations were, however, to a large extent counterbalanced by a more stringent tax policy leading to important areas of cultivation being abandoned before the approach of the tax collector and the gradual impoverishment of the small farmers. The supreme right of the Pharaohs over the country's total resources led to the type of régime usually known as state capitalism. Under this system some raw material industries and almost all manufactured goods, oil, textiles, paper and all mineral products, were declared a royal monopoly. Exploitation of these industries, like the taxes, was let out on a periodic lease to the highest bidder. The beneficiaries of these transactions, both Greek and Egyptian, soon formed a very wealthy, composite bourgeois class capable of stimulating a Graeco-Egyptian form of art and architecture like that at Hermopolis. The only other section of society comparable in power was that of the temples which some of the Ptolemies had been led to favor, in order to secure the loyalty of the priests. Separated intellectually from the Greek administrative class and, also, to a great extent from the impoverished and illiterate common people, the temples developed in strict seclusion a highly intense intellectual life including religious and, to some extent, scientific study.

The same period saw the development of food taboos, the worship of sacred animals, officially considered as living statues of the gods rather than as actual gods, and magic; it also gave rise to the most abstract and esoteric speculations ever to have come into being on the banks of the Nile. As an aid to expression, the priests devised a complex yet richly expressive system of writing, increasing the number of signs from five or six hundred to over three thousand, and making learned combinations of them. They covered the temple walls with these signs, turning them into vast ritual compositions or theological 'sums'.

## Royal theology

Apart from private tombs, all religious architecture was a royal monopoly. Theoretically it was the king alone who built temples. The king alone perpetuated the worship of the gods, his fathers, and it was he alone who reaped the fruits in the form of a long and prosperous life. Thus the monuments were planned to represent his divine connections. The king was not, as in many civilizations, merely the lieutenant or patron of the god or gods. He was god himself. The Egyptians gradually evolved a complex royal theology relating as much to the living person of the king as to his destiny in the other world. The king was identified with the great gods: he was Horus, the falcon god, one of whose eyes was the sun, the other the moon; he was Ra, the sun, whose rays give life to the world; he was Amon, and so on. This identification could be explained and defined by making the king the incarnation of the god, the name Tut-ankhamon, for example, simply means 'living statue of Amon'. But the king was also the son of each of the gods and it was as their son that he built their temples.

Son and successor of the gods, the king was intermediary between heaven and men. Upon the excellence of his connections with the gods depended the state of the country and the progress of the world. Also dependent on the king's life were the flooding of the Nile, the fertility of the earth and the multiplication of flocks: if the king prospered, so did everything, and all collective benefits were transmitted by the king.

Examined in detail, this theology appears to have been one of the spheres in which Egyptian thought advanced most rapidly. Its evolution is difficult to follow, but is essential to the history of architecture, for it reacts not only on the plans of buildings, but also on their style and looks. A few examples will give some idea of this.

Shepsekaf, the successor of Mycerinus, abandoned the pyramidal form (which was readopted by later kings) for his funerary monument and built instead a huge stone mass resembling a gigantic sarcophagus or the tombs of the kings of Dynasties I and II. In the early part of the Eighteenth Dynasty, the pyramidal form was again abandoned, this time almost finally, and the funerary monuments were divided between a temple of the same type as those of the gods and a tomb hollowed out of the mountain a short distance from the temple. Such modifications cannot be attributed merely to a change of taste or formal pattern; they must have been introduced owing to important alterations in the royal theology.

The first really colossal statues appeared during the reign of Amenhotep III; they were often over 60 feet high (instead of measuring between 10 and 20 feet as did their predecessors). The king's funerary temple was also on a much larger scale than those of his predecessors. There is evidence to indicate that about this time a cult of the royal personage was instituted, or of certain of his aspects, considered as a divinity independent of other gods. In the temple of Soleb in the Sudan, the king is portrayed worshipping his own image. The most splendid examples of colossal statues and personal deification of the king date from the period of Ramesses II. It is very tempting to link these two phenomena and to find the explanation for the Colossi of Memnon and the façade of Abu Simbel in this definite change in the concept of royalty, rather than in the desire to express power, or a widespread taste for the colossal. Moreover, in this period, statues of private individuals and royal obelisks adhered to more normal proportions.

## Temple life and ritual

We have seen that it was the king's duty to ensure prosperity for Egypt. He saw to this both by good administration and by the ritual carried out in the temples. As he could not personally officiate at these rites throughout Egypt, his presence was assured by the reliefs on the walls of every temple, showing him carrying out the office. In fact his duties were delegated to priests (who had nothing in common with Christian monks, at least until the late New Kingdom). These priests were ordinary citizens who came to serve the god for one month out of every five or six. During this month of service they conformed to discipline in such matters as dress, food and hygiene. Once it was over they returned to civilian life. Only the high priests of the chief temples served full time and this in no way prevented them from simultaneously carrying out important administrative duties. In exchange for their services they received as payment part of the holy offerings and their posts became hereditary possessions which could even be sold. In the large temples the priests were organized into complex, specialist hierarchies. The offerings to the gods which formed the priests' salaries were provided from land belonging to the temples. The cultivation of this land, the preparation of the offerings, and the manufacture of objects needed for the ritual and for everyday life required a large brigade of agricultural and slave workers. Thus the chief temples were really towns with dwelling houses, workshops, administrative buildings, schools and libraries.

The purpose of the ritual was to shelter, feed and clothe the god, to encourage him ceaselessly to renew the workings of creation whose breakdown would signify the incapacity of the king and result in a final return to the chaos from which the world emerged on the day of creation.

The rite centered on the statue of the god. There were usually two statues of the chief god in a temple. One was permanent, sometimes of

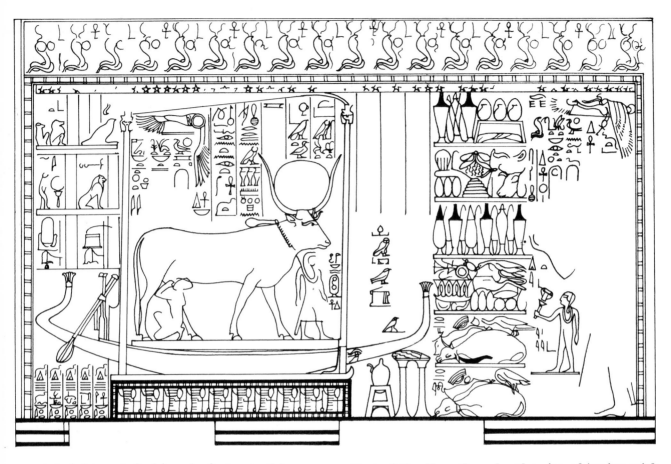

great height and fashioned of stone; this was the focus of the daily ritual. The other was small, made of wood or precious metals, and was placed in a scale model of a boat which could be carried in processions. Statues of minor divinities were placed in subsidiary shrines. In large temples one of the side halls would contain the statues of a series of gods forming the court or ennead of the principal deity. Suitable food had to be provided for the gods to come and inhabit their statues which also had to be animated, after their completion, by means of the ceremony known as the opening of the mouth. The divine presence had to be regularly sustained by allowing the daily penetration of light to the statue and, at times of great festivals, especially that of the New Year, by the rite of 'union with the disc'. The marble statues of the gods were carried either into a room open to the sky or on to the temple roof, and exposed to the rays of the midday sun which endowed them with its divine energy. If all these conditions were fulfilled, the statue became the body of the god and the ritual was effective.

The service of the god was harmonized with the movements of the sun In the Late Period and probably in the time of the New Kingdom as well, it comprised three phases corresponding to the three chief moments of the sun's circuit: its rising, zenith and setting. The morning phase was the most important. Before dawn, the

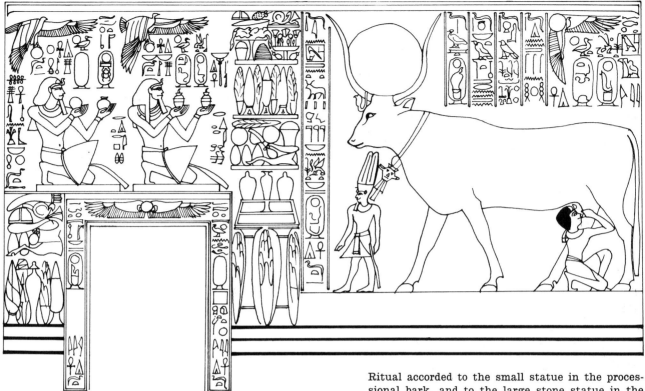

Ritual accorded to the small statue in the processional bark, and to the large stone statue in the main sanctuary (reliefs from the chapel at Deir el Bahari of the goddess Hathor, here represented as a cow)

offerings were prepared in the temple workshops and the priests washed in the sacred lake, purifying their bodies. Then they made the circuit of the temple, pouring water and burning incense to ward off hostile elements. The god's food was next carried in procession to one of the halls of the temple where it was placed on small altars and consecrated. The chief celebrant opened the door of the sanctuary and urged the god to wake. Then, at the moment when the heavenly body, the bearer of life, appeared on the horizon, he opened the doors of the shrine of the god's statue. The newborn light penetrated the god, giving him strength for the new day. Food was placed before the statue along with

an additional offering of a statuette of the goddess Maat, symbol of the cosmic order and of justice on earth. Afterwards the statue was unclothed, washed, dressed afresh, adorned, anointed with oil and incense, and purified. Shrine and sanctuary then remained closed till the following morning. The offerings, after their presentation to the gods, were sometimes placed before the statues of private individuals in one of the outer halls of the temple. The noon rite consisted merely of sprinkling of water and incense burning while the evening ritual involved the renewal of the offerings.

On the chief feast days the movable boat

bearing the statue was carried in procession, sometimes within the temple, in the courtyard or outer sanctuary, sometimes throughout the countryside.

The daily rite was a secret action carried out by a few priests in halls to which they alone had the right of entry. The festivals were public and crowds flocked to them to worship the appearance of the god and to take part in dramatic presentations comparable to the mystery plays of the Middle Ages.

## Mathematics

We are ill prepared to judge the level reached by the Egyptians in mathematics as our knowledge in this field is based on two incomplete papyri and a few fragments, almost all of which date from the Middle Kingdom. These documents are not systematic treatises (such clearly never existed) but a series of problems and answers centering round the workings of fractions, the division of corn according to more or less complicated rules and the computations of areas or volumes, Thus we are in the position of future archaeologists who may have to judge our knowledge with the help of two or three class books of unknown standard, a few student's exercises, and calculations jotted down in the margins of papers or books by a grocer doing his accounts or making a tax return. Supposing the level indicated by our various sources is more or less the same, we may take it to be that attained by a good professional technician, but we may be equally sure that some of their scribes were capable of posing and answering more complex problems. It is easy to calculate the volume of a truncated pyramid or the area of a trapezoid, once the formula has been discovered, but this seems to suggest a geometrical ability superior to that usually attributed to the Egyptians. It is possible that in the learned society of the temples during the Late Period, there may have been fresh progress in mathematics resulting in more abstract speculations than those indicated by the sources available to us which roughly offer the following evidence.

The Egyptians had a system of decimal numbering, with a sign for 1, another for 10, 100, 1000 and so on. To write 654, they had to put down the sign for 100 six times, the sign for 10 five times and that for 1 four times. They used only fractions with a numerator of 1: instead of $\frac{3}{4}$, they had to write $\frac{1}{2}+\frac{1}{4}$. This seemingly complicated system was also normally used by the Greeks (although they knew the system of fractions we now use), the Romans and the Byzantines. With these figures they carried out additions, subtractions, multiplications and divisions, although their multiplications were, in fact, no more than a series of doublings. The principle was based on the fact that every even number is equivalent to the sum of multiples of 2. Thus to multiply 254 by 13 they calculated: 1 x 254=254; 2 x=508; 4 x=1016; 8 x=2032. As 13=8+4+1, all that was needed was to add together the numbers corresponding to 8, 4 and 1: 2032+1016+254=3302.

The Egyptian scribes knew how to square a figure and find its root even if it was a fraction; they did this by employing the rule of three. We have examples of solutions of first degree equations involving an unknown quantity, of second degree equations, of arithmetical progression and of geometrical progression. In geometry the Egyptians knew how to calculate the areas of rectangles, triangles and trapezoids, and the volumes of pyramids and truncated pyramids. They achieved a good approximate formula for the area of a circle, calculating the value of $\pi$ as 3.16, and also for the volumes of cylinders and cones. The following example, which has a direct bearing on architecture, gives an idea of the essential practicality of their problems:

'Method of calculating the sloping side of a

Mathematical problem: find the height of a pyramid
given its base and slope

pyramid whose base is 360 and whose height is 250. You take one half of 360 which is 180; you divide 180 by 250 which equals $\frac{1}{2}+\frac{1}{5}+\frac{1}{50}$ of a cubit. As one cubit equals 7 palms, you multiply by 7. Therefore the sloping side is $5\frac{1}{25}$ palms.' This amounts to determining the slope by the relation of half the base to the height (co-tangent of the base angle). Examination of the pyramids leads one to believe that they had studied the peculiarities of certain simple geometrical figures, that they knew, for inst-ance, about right-angled triangles whose sides measure consecutive figures (3, 4, 5).

## Organization of building sites

If we wish to find out how the building sites were organized, we must first take account of their importance and the number of manual laborers employed on them. No full list of workers has survived, but we have sufficient evidence to give us a very close idea. It is possible, among other things, to calculate the cubic capacity of stone used in building a temple. Let us take as an example that of Medinet Habu which appears to have been the most colossal of the partially preserved temples of the New Kingdom. The main part, the exter-ior of which is decorated with battle scenes dating from the fifth to twelfth year of the reign of Ramesses III, probably took between twelve and fifteen years to build. By a simplified form of calculation we can estimate that it consisted of some 50,000 cubic yards of stone which gives

a daily average of less than twenty cubic yards, corresponding to twenty medium sized blocks. Transport, preparation and laying of the blocks accounted for only a part of the work: this figure, nevertheless, gives adequate proof that the building sites did not employ a large number of workers, probably not more than one thous-and. There is still further proof of this. The village which accommodated most of the work-men employed on the excavation and decoration of the royal tombs consisted of about seventy houses, and the few surviving, incomplete lists of names, rarely exceed two hundred.

With regard to the Pyramids, it was quite different. It was no longer a question of 50,000 cubic yards of stone, but, in the case of the Great Pyramid, over 2,600,000, which would point to a total of about 20,000 or 40,000 men.

The laborers were made up of specialists (quarrymen, stone-cutters, masons, carpenters, draughtsmen, engravers, painters, decorators, goldsmiths and others) who worked all the year round, and non-specialists. We are quite well informed regarding the former as their social standing allowed them to commission or execute statues, stelae or decorated tombs for them-selves which still survive. In the time of the Old Kingdom, the most successful of them were entitled to a mastaba in the cemeteries surround-ing the Pyramids. Under the Middle Kingdom they formed a large proportion of the petit bourgeois class that came into being at the time.

With regard to the state of affairs in the New Kingdom very exact evidence has been discovered in the ruins of the village of Deir el Medineh which housed the workers on the royal tombs. Houses, tombs, letters, accounts, administrative reports, acknowledgements of debts, petty complaints in the local courts, sketches and students' exercises provide a very lively picture of these middle-class state employees who were able to round off their month's wages with private work undertaken for their colleagues. They were paid in kind, but not very generously, were well housed and could ensure just payment by striking if need be. The following extracts are taken from an absentee register:

'Sauadi: the 23rd and 24th of the third month of the flood: at the behest of his superior officer. The 16th of the fourth month: his daughter has her period. The 14th and 15th of the first month of winter: making offerings to the god. The 24th, 25th . . . seeing to the funeral rites of his father.

'Seba: the 17th of the fourth month of the flood: bitten by a scorpion . . . the 27th of the first month of winter: sick.'

In the 29th year of the reign of Ramesses III severe delays in the payment of salaries, in this case food, drove the workers to strike. Here are some extracts from the surviving report:

'The 10th: today the gang went beyond the five walls of the necropolis, saying: "We have been hungry for the past eighteen days." They took up their position behind the funerary temple of Tuthmosis III. The scribe of the necropolis, the two foremen and the two comptrollers came and said to them: "Let us go back (into the temple)," and they took a great oath, saying: "Come, on us Pharaoh's business depends." They spent the day in this place and the night in the necropolis, going as far as the gate of the south wall of the Ramesseum. On the 12th, after sleeping in confusion before the gate, they re-entered the Ramesseum . . . The chief of police left for Thebes saying: "I am going to look for the governor." . . . Hednakht, the scribe of the land-survey, and the priests of the temple heard their complaints: "We are come, driven by hunger and thirst. We have no more clothes, oil, fish or vegetables. Write concerning this to Pharaoh, our master; write to our superior, the chief minister, that they may grant us the wherewithal to live." Then they were given a month's rations.

'The 13th: . . . so spoke Mentumes, chief of police: "Such is my opinion: rise, take up your tools, close your doors, and I will walk before you to the temple of Sety I and will establish you there this morning".'

Two and a half months later, the question was still not settled. Discontent and strikes continued. A month later the problem was still not settled, despite the intervention of the governor and the high priest of Amon.

There is less information regarding the unskilled laborers and it is not known for sure how they were recruited. Pictures of the Hebrews being forced to manufacture bricks for the construction of the Ramesside capital have certainly been responsible for the traditional idea of hordes of prisoners of war and slaves working under the lash of Pharaoh's overseers. This is almost certainly false, though it is true that the Egyptians freely indulged in whipping. There are, however, indications that the two chief sources of workers were the army and statutory labor. In all probability there were insufficient prisoners of war in the time of the Old Kingdom for the construction of the Pyramids. The number of prisoners did not increase until the time of the New Kingdom when the building sites were less important. They seem, however, to have been used for other tasks. A large proportion of them, especially in the early Eighteenth Dynasty, were given as a reward to the soldiers who had captured them or who had particularly distinguished themselves, while others were formed into groups and settled on land which they had to develop to the profit of the gods or the king. The majority of the remainder were handed over to the temples as serfs or slaves, their function being to cultivate the god's land and to execute the bulk of the manual work in the temple workshops. On the walls of one of the tombs near Thebes are portrayed Asiatics building a brick storehouse; they are described as 'booty brought back by His Majesty to work on the Temple of Amon'. We have evidence that a team of sixty Palestinians was employed on the site at Deir el Bahari. Asiatic oxen, too, were used in the quarries and many of the masons had Semitic names. From this it is clear that prisoners and former prisoners took part in the building operations, but only on a small scale. It is possible that the Hebrews, like the Palestinians at Deir el Bahari, joined in the work because of the statutory labor imposed on the colonists who had been compulsorily or voluntarily established in Egypt.

During the Old Kingdom, the army was a small force and levies were made only for a few important campaigns. They could not play a large part in the building of the Pyramids, but saw to the transport and disposition of materials from distant quarries. Under the New Kingdom there was a large standing army, but there were not campaigns every year and we must not exaggerate the warlike activities of the Egyptian conquerors. For instance, Ramesses II, whose reign lasted 67 years, does not appear to have waged war at any time during its last 46 years. Also each campaign lasted only a few months. For the remainder of the time the army was free for other tasks, furnishing the essential part of the labor force needed for the transport of stone between the quarries and the sites and, in particular, for the manipulation of the large blocks required for colossal statues and obelisks. The army also worked on the actual sites. Its leaders and administrators must have had precise knowledge of building techniques. They were asked, for instance, to estimate the number of bricks needed for 'a ramp 1,200 feet long, 90 wide, made up of 120 compartments (?), full of beams . . .100 feet high . . . ' Amenhotep, son of Hapu, who was later worshipped as a god and was probably the builder of the Colossi of Memnon, was chief administrative officer of the army of Amenhotep III. Particular sections of the army appear to have been wholly devoted to public works.

The rest of the manual labor must have been supplied by statutory labor concerning which there is, unfortunately, little information. During the Old Kingdom it is possible that workers were conscripted from all over the country, especially when the flood stopped agricultural work and made the transport of stone easy.

The housing, feeding and equipment of these men clearly formed a complex problem, as there existed no central organization or ministry of public works. Almost every branch of the administration, including the royal estates, the granaries, the treasury, the temples and the army, provided a share for which they were responsible—the labor force, beasts of burden, basic materials, food, clothing, tools and so on. The whole was fairly well co-ordinated by one or more men belonging to one of the organizations concerned, receiving the title of overseer of the works. They were usually high officials or army leaders who also played the parts of architects, engineers and contractors. Sudden changes in authority and subsequent loss of time were probably quite frequent as this letter, one of the earliest to survive and attributable to the Sixth Dynasty, shows:

'The leader of the expedition says: "The letter from the chief minister has been brought to me, bidding me bring the squad of workers (from the quarries) at Turah so that clothing may be distributed in his presence in the precincts of the necropolis. I protest against this assembly at a distant point. As the messenger must come to Turah by boat, I would spend six days at home with the squad before the distribution of the garments. This would be a complete waste, for the loss of a single working day would be enough to clothe the squad"'.

The majority of the laborers engaged on the construction of the Pyramids did not work full time but according to a rota, probably monthly. The building sites were split up into two or four sectors in each of which the squads of workers were again subdivided. In the time of the New Kingdom only the division into two sectors, left and right, was kept. A highly developed system of accounts was established for every branch of the work, in which can be seen the ancient Egyptians' love of bureaucracy. Almost every stone was 'signed' by the squad responsible; a daily record of the number of men at each point of the site, the number of stones moved or erected and the volume of earth banked up, was inscribed on papyri, slivers of limestone or shards of pottery. The following is an account concerning the construction of a building that formed part of the temple of Sety I at Abydos: 'The 22nd of the third month of winter: account of work carried out by the laborers' squad of the left: they have raised from the quay of the palace of Sety I which is to the south of the temple (called) "Sety I is bountiful to Osiris": various blocks of stone: 29; bases of columns: 3; paving stones: 3; a total of 35 different blocks of stone. They have unloaded stones in the same place: from boats under the command

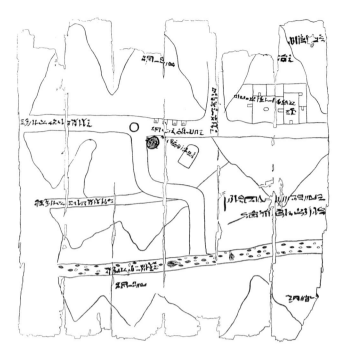

Map, drawn on papyrus, showing mineral deposits in the mountains in the east of Egypt

of Inhermes: $2\frac{1}{2}$ cargoes, or 12 stones; from boats under the direction of the carrier, Penimen: 4 cargoes or 7 blocks and 8 paving stones: total 15; grand total: $6\frac{1}{2}$ cargoes or 27 blocks.'

Here are extracts from another account for a temple of the Eighteenth Dynasty, probably that at Deir el Bahari:

'The 3rd of the second month of the flood: attendance this day:
Those who do carpentry work: 16 men.
Those who hew flagstones for the ceiling: 6.
Those who are in the hypostyle: 2.
Those who work on the quartzite statue: 7.
Those who set up the flagstones for the ceiling: 4 . . .
Engravers: 20.
Overseers: 2 . . .'

# Plates

## Temple of Mentuhotep at Deir el Bahari

67   View from the cliff. In the left background is the south retaining wall of the first terrace of the temple of Hatshepsut and, in the center, the courtyard of the temple of Mentuhotep. The series of circles marks the site of trenches planted with trees. Center, the remains of the double pedestal of the pyramid. Foreground, the courtyard and hypostyle hall preceding the small sanctuary in the cliff. The excavation in the middle of this last section leads to one of the two vaults. (See also plate 78.)

## Pavilion of Sesostris I at Karnak

68-   The pillars are decorated with scenes showing the
72    king making offerings to the god Amon who is usually represented (68, 69, 71, 72) as a man wrapped in a shroud, raising a phallus, his head topped by two goose quills. This is basically the guise of the god Min, here considered as one of the aspects of Amon. On the outside of the balustrade are carved allegorical representations of the various regions (68, 71) together with their areas and the normal level of the Nile flood in their territory (70). In the center of the building is a pedestal (71) on which the god's bark was placed in the processional courtyard. It is later than the rest of the building (c.1800), and is usually supposed to replace a double throne on which the king was recrowned at his jubilee, but this does not exclude the possibility that the pavilion was always a form of altar and that the pedestal replaced a similar feature. The rain water was conducted from the roof by a spout in the shape of a lion (68). Behind the pavilion may be seen the remains of the great boundary wall of Karnak built of brick according to a complicated technique.

## Pavilion of Amenhotep I at Karnak

73   Many of the alabaster blocks of this building were rediscovered in bad condition with chipped edges. The restored portions are lighter than the original and easily distinguishable: the upper edge of the cornice, in particular, had to be completely reconstructed. (See also plate 72.)

## Tomb of Sarenput II at Aswan

74   The morning light penetrates to the back of the tomb causing the terminal niche to stand out with striking effect.

## Fortress of Buhen.

75   From right to left: the ditch, the glacis, the first wall with its rows of loopholes (originally there were three) and semicircular bastions (the remains of one of which can be seen in the center), and the main wall with its rectangular bastions.

## Temple of Hatshepsut at Deir el Bahari

76-   The temple from the front. The first colonnade was
77    faultily restored, resulting in a difference in height between the right and left sectors: the latter is too low.

78   The rocky amphitheatre of Deir el Bahari. Behind the temple of Hatshepsut are the ruins of the temple of Mentuhotep. Between the rear or western sections of the two temples may be distinguished a few columns belonging to a sanctuary of Tuthmosis III, recently discovered by Professor Dobrowski.

79   One of the Hathor-head or sistrum columns of the chapel of the goddess Hathor.

80   Façade of the chapel of the god Anubis. Note the extreme irregularity of the masonry and the way the architraves rest on the columns.

81   A feature of the protodoric colonnade, so called because of the resemblance of its polygonal columns to those of the Doric style.

82   Ceiling of one of the sanctuaries on the northern side of the second terrace. Some of the sanctuaries of this temple have kept their colors almost intact. The tops of the side walls are ornamented with a frieze of cobras and symbolic hieroglyphs representing life, stability, etc. The vault is, technically speaking, sham, being formed of slabs hollowed out to form a semicircle: it is decorated with stars.

**Temples of Chephren at Giza**
Plan of upper and lower temples 1:1,500

Longitudinal and cross sections of the lower temple o

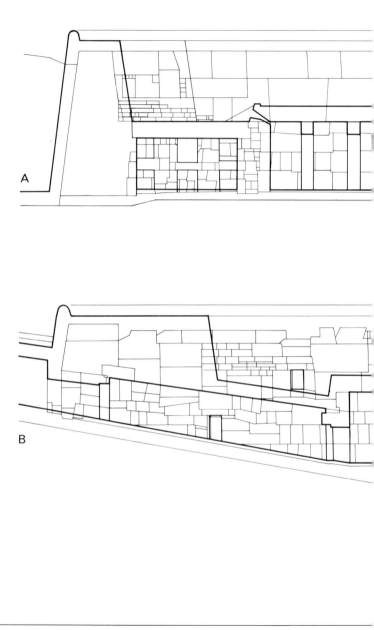

A

B

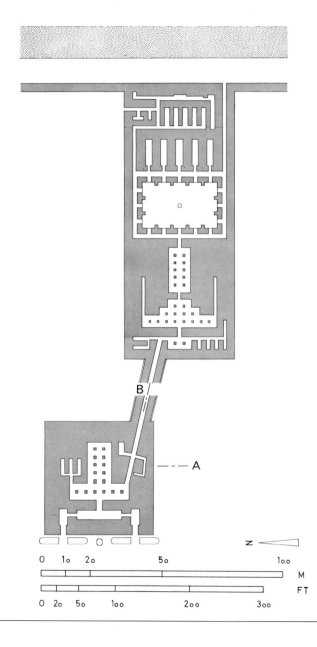

B

A

N

0  1o  2o        5o              1oo

M

FT

0  2o  5o    1oo            2oo            3oo

hephren 1:300

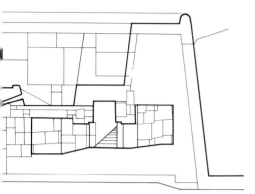

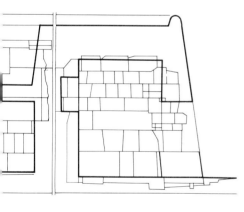

## Pyramid of Unas at Saqqara
Plan of the descent and chambers 1:600

## Mastaba of Mereruka at Saqqara
Plan of the tomb 1:600

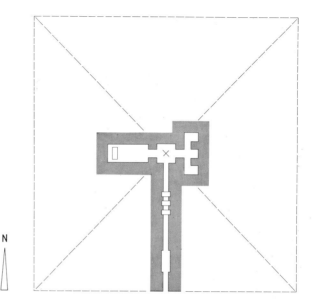

N

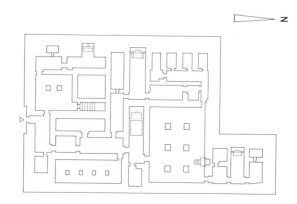

N

# Notes

## Temple of Mentuhotep at Deir el Bahari

Eleventh Dynasty (c.2050). Mentuhotep was Prince of Thebes before he reunified the country; his tomb complex is very different from those of the kings of the Old Kingdom. It is similar to the tombs of most of the princes of the First Intermediary Period and consists of a chapel buried in the cliff preceded by a courtyard; under the chapel is a vault. Like the royal tombs it includes a reception temple, which is not free-standing, and a pyramid. The latter, however, no longer shelters the body of the sovereign and, to some extent, serves as a symbol of royalty; it stands on a vast pedestal divided into two levels, both surrounded by a colonnade.

## Pavilion of Sesostris I at Karnak

Twelfth Dynasty (c. 1950). This small building has been reconstructed in the north-west corner of the precinct at Karnak; detached fragments of it were found among the foundations of the Third Pylon of the great temple built by Amenhotep III, c.1400; he had made fresh use of the blocks as constructional materials. The building is wholly composed of fine limestone and contains an exceptionally fine series of reliefs of great iconographic interest. Contrary to the usual procedure they were probably not heightened by the use of color; there are only slight traces of this on the upper cornice.

## Pavilion of Amenhotep I at Karnak

Eighteenth Dynasty (c. 1550). Like that of Sesostris I, discovered in fragments embedded in the foundations of the Third Pylon of the great temple. It has also been reconstructed in the north-west corner of the precinct. The building is wholly composed of blocks of alabaster. As information concerning it is still unpublished, it has not been possible to include the plan. It was probably erected within the temple at Karnak to house the bark of the god in normal circumstances. Its position inside a large hall explains the difference between its proportions and those of its present-day neighbor.

## Tomb of Sarenput II at Aswan (Tomb No. 31)

Twelfth Dynasty (c.1900). The tomb of Sarenput, governor of the province of Aswan, must have been constructed in the reign of Sesostris II. It consists of a long staircase climbing the cliff, and a courtyard open to the sky: within the rock is an antechamber with six pillars followed by a corridor ornamented with statues of the dead man in niches, and a chapel with four pillars terminating in another niche containing a statue of the dead man in diorite.

## Fort at Buhen

Twelfth Dynasty. One of the best preserved and most important Egyptian fortresses of the Middle Kingdom, in course of excavation by an English team under the direction of Professor Emery. As the work is not yet finished, it is not possible to include plans here. The system of fortification bears a strange resemblance to that of European medieval castles. It consists of a ditch, a first line of defence with a sloping glacis, a wall with loopholes facing different directions strengthened here and there with semicircular bastions, and a second line of defence formed by a high wall reinforced by rectangular towers.

## Funerary Temple of Hatshepsut at Deir el Bahari

Eighteenth Dynasty (c. 1500). The temple was built under the direction of Senmut, the governor of the domains of Amon, in the same rocky amphitheatre as that of Mentuhotep, slightly to the north of it. It has a lower court, the back of which is a colonnade serving as a retaining wall for the first terrace which is reached by a long ramp. On the east this terrace is bounded by the retaining colonnade of the second terrace and by two lateral sanctuaries, the one on the north dedicated to the god Anubis, that on the south to the goddess Hathor. Its northern boundary is formed by another colonnade, known as the protodoric, which holds the rubble of the cliff in check. A fresh ramp leads to the second terrace which is bordered by a series of statues of the queen bearing the attributes of the god Osiris. The center of this terrace is occupied by a pillared courtyard or great hall and at each side are subsidiary shrines. The principal shrine is set on the axis of the temple and is hollowed out of the cliff.

81

**Funerary temple of Mentuhotep at Deir el Bahari**
Plan and elevation 1:1,500

**Pavilion of Sesostris I at Karnak**
Plan and profile 1:300

**Tomb of Sarenput at Aswan (No. 31)**
Cross section and plan 1:500

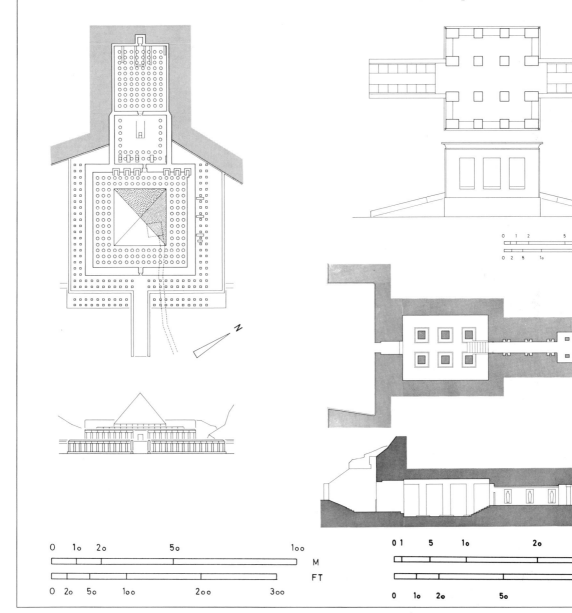

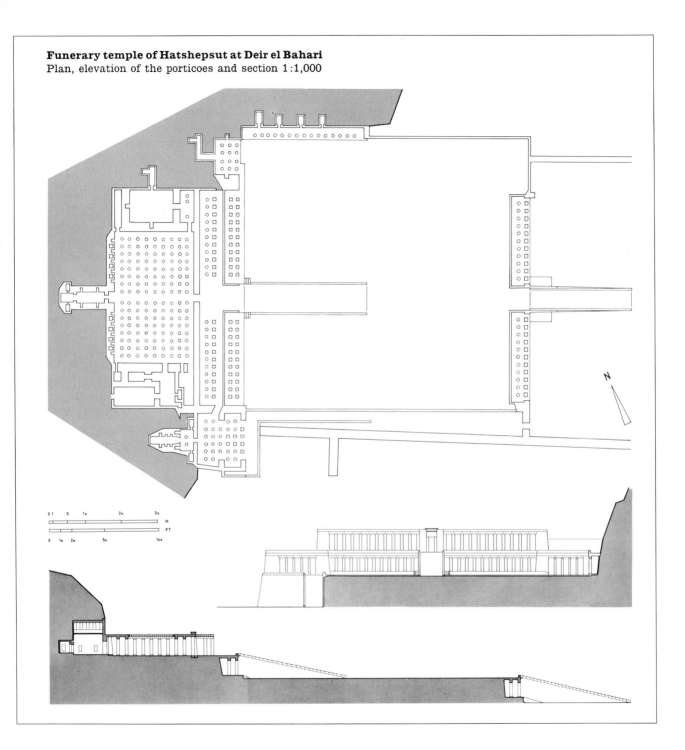

**Funerary temple of Hatshepsut at Deir el Bahari**
Plan, elevation of the porticoes and section 1:1,000

0 1  5  1o      2o        3o
M
FT
0  1o  2o    5o          1oo

# 2. Aims of Egyptian Architecture

## Forms and functions

The governing preoccupations of the architecture of our own age—the relationship between form and function, and constructional techniques—afford a means of approach to the study of Egyptian architecture. First we must analyze the functional aspect and try to discover what aim the Egyptians had in mind when they built their pyramids and temples. This function had both a practical and a religious aspect. From the practical point of view, the pyramids were tombs; the temples, places of worship. The connection between this practical function and the forms of the buildings seems to have been much the same in Egypt as in other civilizations, but there is a great difference in the case of the religious functions. Therefore, these are examined first.

The biggest difference between the architecture of the Egyptians and our own lies in the fact that the desired spiritual effect of Egyptian forms was, to a great extent, based on their symbolic content. This idea of symbolism can be defined in many ways and is difficult to grasp. For our purpose, a building is symbolic when it attempts to evoke or reproduce elements which, from our point of view, are irrelevant to it. In this way, it attaches to itself the feelings and ideas which are linked to these elements in the minds of its creators and beholders, or, according to a more primitive form of reasoning, it appropriates the forces contained in these elements. Here we come up against a form of expression to which we are unaccustomed. Nevertheless, we may find examples in Western art, ranging from the cruciform plans of most churches to the play of light in Le Corbusier's chapel at Ronchamp.

## Architecture and aesthetic

Obviously, the relationship of surfaces and the arrangement of interior space produce an atmosphere, a sensation of harmony, grandeur, contemplation or isolation, or perhaps a feeling of communion with nature, a sense of movement or immobility. These, however, are all psychological reactions, not always easily distinguishable from aesthetic ones. The Egyptian architects made use of this type of reaction but, as with other aesthetic factors, merely as a reinforcement of the potency of the symbols and the power of the temple. The beauty of the building indicated the characteristic of divinity and helped to transform it from a mere human construction into the image of the celestial horizon, ensuring its participation in the superhuman order and encouraging the generosity of the god. Only after the Egyptian gods had checked the aesthetic side of the temple destined for them, did they condescend to come and dwell there. 'When the great winged scarab (the sun) rises from the primordial ocean and sails through the heavens in the guise of Horus . . . he stops in the heaven before this temple and his heart is filled with joy as he looks at it. Then he becomes one with his statue, in his favorite place . . . he is satisfied with the monument that the king . . . has erected for him.' The texts describing the temples are full of words that may be translated by beauty, beautiful, magnificent, superb, sumptuous, and so on. Very often, however, a religious or quantitative shade of meaning is added to the predominant aesthetic sense. Beauty was always present in the minds of the builders, but, it must be stressed, merely as a contributory factor. It is easy enough for us to comprehend this subordination of beauty as, for many of our own architects, it is only a by-product of buildings whose functions are determined by mechanical criteria. First, then, we can concentrate on the symbolic nature of Egyptian architecture, especially that of the temples, concerning which we possess surer knowledge.

## Architectural symbolism

An Egyptian temple was the place which the god came to inhabit (in his statue), where he was fed, clothed and protected; it was his castle. If Egyptian speculations had stopped there, the temples would have been no more than idealized houses or palaces, built of stone so as to become eternal like the god and slightly adapted to facilitate his service; but there would have been little question of symbolism. The Egyptians, however, also regarded this house of the god as the materialization of the celestial horizon from which he emerged to bring light to the world—this is the image that recurs most frequently in texts of all periods—and of the primordial earth which first emerged, after the act of creation, from original chaos (primordial ocean), on which the first of the gods supported himself to pursue his creative work. The temple, the dwelling place of the god, had to represent both the world and a divine palace; the temple was a stage on which was enacted the meetings between god and the king as representative of the people of

The temple of Denderah depicted in the center of the horizon and bathed in the rays of the sun which the goddess of the heavens brings forth in the morning

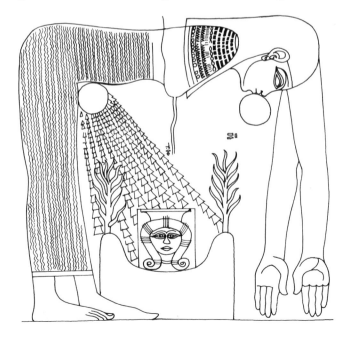

Egypt. So it became a microcosm of Egypt and the entire cosmos where this encounter of god with man actually took place. This concept may be found in many other civilizations and plays a key part in Egyptian architecture. It is seldom found explicitly set out in texts dating from before the Late Period; there is, however, a very ancient ritual of the 'laying of the first stone', copied in the Eighteenth Dynasty from an original dating from the early Old Kingdom.

The decoration of the temples, the ceilings covered with stars, for instance, also clearly stemmed from the Old Kingdom. Many other types of symbolic representation were used. These included the reproduction of ancient prehistoric sanctuaries whose forms were often borrowed for the shrine of the god; the evocation of sacred objects associated with one or other of the gods; the use of the symbolic values of different materials including stones, metals such as gold, the flesh of the gods, or the symbol of life, or of colors—green or black, for instance, were colors indicating rebirth; the use of hieroglyphics in the decoration—signs of 'life' or 'force', or 'stability', arranged in the friezes; the transposition of a mechanical function to a religious or magic plane—a gargoyle scatters the enemies of the god, just as it serves to draw off the rainwater. Such symbolism impregnated the entire temple, giving shape to, or at any rate clarifying, all its details. A single feature could evoke a multiplicity of forms, myths, or spiritual forces, and it is often impossible to know which images have influenced its shape or place in the architecture and which are no more than later commentaries.

However complex and varied this symbolism may have been, it obeyed simple laws. Each symbol had to be an evocation of an episode in the god's career, the scene of one of his exploits, his nature, or one of his attributes, and it was the purpose of these evocations to facilitate the renewal of his acts or the consolidation of his power. If we try to make the temples into idealizations of the human form, or the pyramids into secret repositories of infinite scientific or esoteric knowledge, we are completely on the wrong track.

Among peoples with a less developed sense of stylization and abstraction, a similar development of symbolic theories might have produced a strange form of natural theology where sham trees and rocks would have been surmounted by statues of strange divinities similar to the human beings with animal heads pictured in the reliefs of the royal tombs. In Egypt, these symbols were either carved in low relief or were embodied in very simple architectural features which were no more than stylized allusions to the spiritual forces it was their duty to contain. The temple precincts contained many buildings—the principal temple, secondary chapels, processional altars; in the later temples was accommodation for lying-in, outbuildings for business use and so on; all were arranged with regard to ritualistic, religious and aesthetic standards about which we know little, as none of these complexes has been sufficiently well preserved. They also always included a sheet of water known as the sacred lake. On these lakes grew plants which also played their part in theology. The papyrus represented the marsh where Isis took refuge to give birth to her son, Horus, and the lotus the flower that sprang from primordial chaos to support the young sun with his creative powers. The basins were surrounded by trees; other plants formed groves, bordered the avenues, and sometimes grew round the courts of the temple. They were not there merely to enliven the landscape: certain varieties had direct connections with particular gods, mythological episodes, or religious centers. Apart from references in the texts to this symbolic form of landscaping, only scanty traces remain, including the sacred lakes of

Karnak, Medinet Habu and Denderah, some hollows in the ground, as at the temple of Mentuhotep at Deir el Bahari and a few representations on temples and private tombs.

## Harmony of temple design with landscape

The extraordinary harmony between the overall forms of Egyptian monuments and the landscape has frequently been stressed. The temples, with their simple shapes, extended proportions and clean, horizontal rooflines, echo the calm progression and dominating horizontal lines of the cliffs, particularly those to the west of the Nile, which border the valley south of Cairo. Much has been made of this harmony by those who believe that the topography of a country has a wide influence on the architecture of its inhabitants. It is, however, difficult to use Egypt as an example, for it is impossible to know in this case how much is unconscious influence and how much intentional imitation. We have just seen that the Egyptians were at least aware of this resemblance, but it is uncertain whether it was an effect sought after from the start of their civilization, thus contributing to the formation of the basic formal structures of Pharaonic architecture—the most ancient remains, tombs of the Thinite Period, already reveal these tendencies, but their religious background is unknown—or whether it was merely proven and exploited symbolically. Once this form of building was created, reference to its topographical significance becomes useless: each temple can be explained by its relationship to previous ones, quite independent of any geographical influence. In a few extreme cases, however, this is not possible, and I have selected the two most obvious as examples of how this type of symbolism can be formally applied.

The funerary temple of Queen Hatshepsut at Deir el Bahari is the most famous example of an

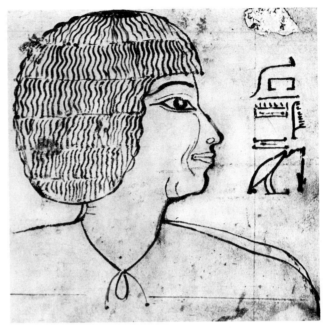

Portrait of Senmut, architect of Deir el Bahari (sketched on a wall of his tomb)

architecture adapted to its natural surroundings. In a wide amphitheatre formed by the cliff whose abrupt drop is broken by fallen rocks, lies a superimposition of three long colonnades of polished stone, the uppermost of which has to a large extent crumbled away. These colonnades echo the drop of the cliff; the ramps and what is left of the terraces are related to the fallen rocks. Many commentators have taken this exceptional harmony to be proof of a completely aesthetic outlook regarding the siting and form of monuments. Others, however, have realized the danger of crediting the ancients with a preoccupation more in line with the spirit of the twentieth century than with the more primitive mentality of pre-Greek antiquity, and consider this harmony between nature and architecture to be unconscious. The architect Ricke was probably the first to accentuate correctly the relationship between the cosmic symbol and this adaptation to the landscape. The exterior of the temple at Deir el Bahari only echoes the dominant lines of the Egyptian landscape in a very general, diffuse manner; like most of the other temples it freely integrates itself with a predetermined part of the landscape. The beauty of its severe lines increases the divine nature of the section of the mountain formed by the temple. Thus, this harmony with the setting, which we regard as an aesthetic achievement, has been consciously worked out, but for theological rather than architectural reasons.

The finest of the rock temples, and the most interesting from the point of view of their integration with the landscape, are those which Ramesses II had constructed for himself and Queen Nefertari in the mountain of Abu Simbel. As in the case of Deir el Bahari, this mountain must have been the object of special veneration. The façades of the two temples are constructed so as scarcely to break its lines. Many other rock temples include an exterior colonnade or a pylon, but, at Abu Simbel, these features are wholly contained within the mountain. On the front of the great temple of Ramesses II are four huge statues of the king, carved in the massive rock, and apparently backed by a smooth wall. The whole composition freely evokes the pylons that stand at the entrances of temples, in front of which statues of the king were erected. Instead of pushing back the wall on either side of the statues to give them their full effect and complete the evocation of the pylon, the Egyptians let the mountain enfold them. In the case of the small temple, the aim is made even more clear: the pilasters separating the large statues of the king and queen are not set vertically and in recession, but are inclined so that they carry on the slope of the mountain as far as possible. The wish to integrate the temples with the rock is clearly expressed. As at Deir el Bahari, the mountain is also part of the temples, endowing them with its power and its sacred character.

As we have already seen, each feature of a temple was conditioned and explained by an entire network of symbols: some influenced its shape, some merely its decoration, and others, again, were no more than added glosses. To illustrate this, let us take pylons and pillars.

## Pylons

The pylon did not appear as a feature of Egyptian architecture until the beginning of the New Kingdom. It is a monumental gateway composed of two massive blocks with inclined walls, united by a door whose coping is about half their height. They were, as a rule, decorated with great wooden masts, sometimes twice their height, from whose summits pennants floated in the breeze. Several religious images are frequently associated with these features. The first is the horizon, which the Egyptians represented as a pass between two mountains, in which the sun would appear. Similarly, the rising sun appears between the two towers of

A pylon, after a New Kingdom relief

the pylon, which is theoretically orientated towards the east, to bring light to the temple and penetrate as far as the sanctuary. This association between the pylon-horizon and the sun is given concrete form in the imitation pylon at Abu Simbel where the sculptured image of Ra, the sun god, surmounts the door.

In the second place, the two towers of the pylon are identified with Isis and Nephthys, the two sisters of Osiris, who watch over his body. The speculations centering round the sun and the legend of Osiris clearly assisted the formation of this image, which then easily became connected with the previous one. Again, being the entrance gate of the temple, the pylon had to defend the doorway against hostile forces. Lastly, as the horizon from which the sun appears, it is the throne of the god or the king and so became the setting for the ceremony of the coronation of the god.

## Supports

The pillars of the temples were the features which best lent themselves to the interplay of symbols; their shapes could be varied more easily than those of walls or roofs. Their function as supports related them to the pillars which were supposed to hold up the vault of heaven, just as they carried the weight of the roof of the temple whose ceiling was painted with stars. Each column of the temple could be associated with one of the gods who, according to the myths, bore the weight of the heavens—Shu, for instance, who, from the time of creation, separated heaven from earth. The pillars could represent one of the Egyptian plants: the palm, the papyrus, or the lotus, each of which had a very distinctive symbolic aura. The palm was associated with the town of Buto, a very important center of religion especially at the end of the prehistoric period, the papyrus represented Lower Egypt, and the lotus was the support of the young sun at the time of the creation. The

groups of pillars in the colonnades were evocative of vegetation in general, or the marshy trails bordering the greater part of the Nile valley at the edge of the cultivated zone. In the Late Period, there was a great increase in this type of floral capital and they became more intricate; the columns of one hall could represent a highly complex piece of religious iconography. The great hypostyle hall at Esna, the only part of the temple to survive, was frequently compared to a thicket of papyrus. Other texts in this hall explain the significance of the various floral columns by an assonance between the name of the plant represented on the capital and that of a god or a divine quality. For the Egyptians the essence of a being resided in his name; what to us is no more than a fairly bad pun, was, for them, a theological explanation. Two homonyms, even if they were only approximate, were bound to be related. Thus we read 'He modeled (nb) the floral (nbty) column for the master (nb) of the potter's wheel'. It is difficult to know whether the appearance of the columns was responsible for this word-play, or whether the word-play determined the choice of capitals.

The capital could be a more direct evocation of a divinity. In the temples dedicated to the goddess Hathor, so-called Hathor-head pillars or columns were almost always used. The capitals of these reproduce on one, two, or four faces, the head of the goddess, Hathor, with its cows' horns, surmounted by a small building. This is the shape which is usually given to the musical instrument known as the sistrum, a kind of rattle, which played a great part in the worship of the goddess. The temple built by Nectanebo at Hermopolis was 'the resting-place of his mother, Useret-Nehemet-auy . . . each of the eight sistrums that it contains is for Hathor-Nehemet-auy. It is the resting-place of the eight primordial genies . . . and the columns of fine white stone in front of this temple, each comprising four representations of a sistrum plated with gold . . .'. From this it seems that the façade of this temple, of which nothing remains, must have been composed of eight (or two) Hathor-head columns which were themselves sacred objects, chosen to represent the eight genies of creation around whom the entire cosmogony of this religious center developed.

There was an even more direct evocation in the Osiride pillars which were probably in use in the Old Kingdom, but are found particularly in the courtyards of the Ramesside temples. They were never used in the interior of temples. At Abu Simbel, for instance, they form part of the decoration of the first hall, but this played the part of a courtyard in the liturgy, as the decoration shows. These pillars disappeared before the Late Period; they were colossal statues of the Pharaoh represented with the attributes of Osiris, placed against a pillar and fulfilling no architectural function. As far as I know, there has been no satisfactory explanation of their theological significance.

## Lighting

These columns, walls, and reliefs were brought to life by light. After a temple was completed, it was subjected, at any rate in the time of the Late Period, to the ceremony of the opening of the mouth, as if it were a dead body or a statue. Like the statue within, the temple had to be brought back to life every morning by the light, which had then to penetrate the sanctuary to bring the god to life. Thus, the light was not merely the power of illumination, it was the divine emanation of the sun god. This precious force was the object of the entire attention of the architect who took care that it penetrated to the gods in the best possible way, ensuring the correct balance of the light of life and the shadow of mystery. The nature of the god was impenetrable and invisible; he had to remain surrounded by shadows. Now it becomes possible for us to realize the architectural significance of this conception which wholly conditioned the organization of interior space. If we lose sight of this, we expose ourselves to serious interpretative errors which are made all the more easy as the result of the ruined state of most of the temples. A critic as acute as Bruno Zevi, for example, has classified the temples at Karnak and Luxor as monuments in which vertical lines are completely predominant. Such an impression is given easily enough by an isolated column or an entire hall whose pillars point skywards, the ceiling and most of the architraves having disappeared. The eye is automatically drawn upwards by the light and rests on a number of verticals. When the roof was still in position, when most of the columns were plunged in semi-darkness and the light led one's eye on to further halls, the impression received was completely different. The Egyptians were well aware how to organize the interior lighting of their monumental buildings by creating axes of light, directing beams like theatrical spotlights on to a statue, leaving one room in shadow, and gradually increasing the darkness to suggest the rising mystery. In the central hall of the lower temple of Chephren, almost life-size statues in black stone, including the famous one of the Pharaoh with the falcon, were set along the wall between the pillars. Light filtered through narrow windows arranged at the junction of walls and ceiling, was directed on to all the statues and spread through the hall by reflection from the polished alabaster floor; the red granite pillars and walls remained in shadow. This interplay of light and shade helped to concentrate attention on the statues and brought the stiff lines of the hall to life in a somewhat theatrical manner. In the tomb of Sarenput at Aswan, the disposition of the light is ordered by more simple means. Starting from the door which is orientated towards the east, the light is gently directed towards the statue of the dead man which is placed in the niche at the rear of the tomb; every line converges upon it as the result of the perspective, the narrowing walls and rising ground after the central flight of steps, and the inward curve of the ceiling in the second half of the corridor. The softly-lit walls become progressively more indistinct and the niche better lit, because it faces the source of light and stands out in the semi-darkness. Everything not directly in the sloping approach to the statue remains in shadow.

## Formal vocabulary

It is possible to express this complex symbolism in an extremely simple architectural vocabulary, richer than that of the Greeks, but, nevertheless, comprising only a very limited number of possible forms. We shall do no more than recall the basic features, almost all of which we have already met.

Except in special cases—evocations of prehistoric sanctuaries, for instance—religious buildings always had terraced roofs and horizontal ceilings. There is ample evidence that vaulted ceilings were employed in all periods, but, in religious architecture, their use remained limited and, in every case, had to correspond to an exact symbolic idea. Walls were set at right angles, their faces either vertical or slightly inclined. The inner face was usually vertical, the outer, inclined. There were only two types of coping for walls and buildings: either they were rounded or had a slight cornice. The angles of the walls were frequently reinforced by a torus molding, a thin cylinder partially set in the masonry, stressing the start of the cornice which often surmounted door lintels. The pillars were the features which contributed most to characterizing the interior style of each period, and could assume a great range of shapes. They could be geometrical—square or rectangular, circular, octagonal, or up to sixteen-sided, uniform or dissimilar, fluted or plain, cylindrical or gradually narrowing towards the top—or they could be reminiscent of a plant or a religious object such as the sistrum. Plants could be represented by the whole column with the shaft as the stem, or merely by the capital symbolizing the leaves and flowers. Except in the Late Period when regular cylindrical shafts were surmounted by capitals bearing an infinite variety of plants arranged in bunches, the number represented was very limited; the palm, papyrus in flower or in bud, and the lotus were usually the only ones employed.

The symbolic significance of each of these features could be amplified by decoration and lighting. Most of them can be traced back to the old architecture of wood, reeds, clay, or bricks. The concave cornice must have been a stylization of the ribs of palm leaves and the fluted columns a recollection of beams hollowed with the chisel.

## Applications of 'symbolism'

To summarize the symbolism of the temples, to gain a proper understanding of the relationship between the intentions of the ancient architects and the forms chosen to embody them, and to see how they combined the elements of this vocabulary, it is best to take Edfu as an example, as it is the best preserved of all the temples of Egypt. There is no longer any trace of the great brick wall which shut off the natural world from the superhuman world; of the group of buildings set in the enclosure all that survives, apart from the great temple, is the main section of the Birth House; nothing remains of the so-called theological landscape. Nor is anything left of the colors which lent emphasis to the sculptured decoration, enlivening the stones which are now as gray and gloomy as those of the buildings of our own large towns. Nevertheless, the shapes of the monumental buildings and the basic features of the interior lighting are preserved. Access to the temple is now from the rear. From this angle it appears as an elongated mass made to seem more squat because of its slightly sloping walls; the horizontal coping is exaggerated by the cornice surmounting it, and the angles of the building are rounded by use of the torus molding. The monotonous array of carvings, set in horizontal bands, adds still further to the impression of stiffness given by the long, blind wall, uninterrupted by a single vertical; there are only two small doors in the vast front and these are scarcely visible. This long blockhouse is supported by the double mass of the pylon with its sloping walls, which is both wider and higher than the rest of the temple. The whole building gives an impression of powerful solidity, and a sense of enclosure which is almost hostile. The exterior wall plays the part of the first fortified wall of a fortress; it is separated from the temple by a ring corridor, hemmed in by two sheer walls and defended by gargoyles in the shape of lions. The calm, extended lines of the entire composition, dominated by the pylon, resemble those of the surrounding countryside, particularly the cliff which dominates the valley at a distance. Similarly, the two towers of the pylon echo two of the peaks of the Arabian range beyond the cliff, between which it is possible to see the sun appear each morning. Once past the pylon, we are in an entirely different world: an almost square courtyard bordered on three sides by a colonnade whose heavy entablature brings the upward sweep to a halt. The fourth side is formed by the façade of the enclosed portion of the temple. This has an entablature with a cornice which cuts a clean horizontal line against the sky, and is supported by two sloping walls and six columns whose high abaci allow the capitals to stand out clearly against the dark background of the hall. The spaces between these columns are filled in to about half their height by low walls. The stiff unfolding of long, horizontal walls is replaced by a sense of balance between the light and the intercolumniations in the shadow, between the vegetable elements—the capitals evoking the various plants of Egypt—

and those shaped geometrically. This harmonious space, flooded with sunlight and devoted to the celebration of festivals, is symbolic of Egypt coming to worship the god Horus of Edfu. This symbolism is specially explained in the decoration where the gods of the different regions are shown in geographical order, coming to pay homage to their fellow divinity.

At the door of the first hypostyle hall, there is another change of atmosphere. From this point, the light gradually fades, leading the eye on up the axis of the temple which is more lit than the rest, towards the central sanctuary where the god watches in his shrine. The light decreases in the successive halls in proportion to the lowering of the ceiling and the raising of the floor; the close-set columns and the ever-narrower doors prevent the visitor from departing from this axis. This central opening filled with light is the manifestation of the path of the sun to the statue. This impression of growing mystery and ascent towards the divinity is now nowhere as powerful as at Edfu, but it must have been the predominant feature of the interior arrangement of almost every temple. This magnificent piece of production was not an aesthetic ordering of interior space for the benefit of the human spectator; it was an arrangement for the surroundings of the god. The first hall was no more than an introduction to the mysterious world inhabited by the god. It did not form part of the round of the daily ritual and was brought to life only at the time of festivals; thus the orientation of the light is not as strictly observed as in the following halls. Once the visitor leaves the axis of the temple, he finds himself in an area where the light is no longer orientated. It enters, more or less freely, through the upper part of the façade, illuminating the bases as much as the upper portions of the columns. Eyes are directed to the floral capitals and are attracted by their variety. Despite the horizontal registers of the decoration, the vertical lines are clearly predominant; they suggest a burst of plant life. In the second hall we are completely held by the orientation towards the sanctuary to which everything else is sacrificed. The center aisle is lit by openings in the ceiling, the side aisles remain in shadow, and the shafts of the columns, with their lightly swollen bases, seem heavier than those of the first hall and all the more effectively forbid one's attention to wander. The capitals are either in shadow or outlined against the light. So we come to the central sanctuary: this is separated from the minor ones surrounding it by an ambulatory which resembles the exterior ring corridor in its narrowness and the way in which it is shut in. Thus isolated and finally defended, the sanctuary, with its sloping walls, its corner moldings, its cornice, and its own ceiling, stands like an independent temple of which it is a summary, just like the shrine within it. In this case the shrine has a pyramidal coping directly recalling the sacred stone of the sun at Heliopolis where it formed a receptacle for the falcon god traversing the heavens like the sun of which he was one of the manifestations.

In the case of the temples, texts allow us to have a fairly certain idea of the chief kinds of symbolism and their connection with the forms of the buildings, but this is not so regarding the pyramids. We know that they were the tombs of the Pharaohs of the Old and Middle Kingdoms, and the centers of their funerary cults, and we may deduce that they were a grandiose means of exalting the Pharaoh, both after his death and during his lifetime. In my opinion, a form of worship was held in the Pharaoh's lifetime, just as in the so-called funerary temples of the New Kingdom. We need to know, however, why such forms were selected to express this exaltation of monarchy and why, especially, the Egyptians graduated from the step pyramid of Zoser to the true pyramids of Sneferu and Cheops. Here it is clearly possible to give an authentic explana-

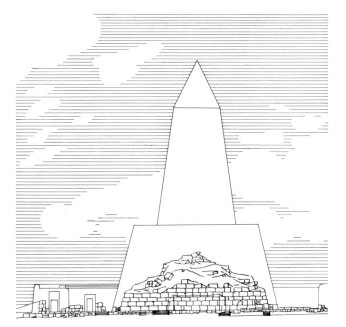

Sun temple of Neuser-ra (reconstruction by Borchardt)

tion: with the adoption of stone, the Egyptians developed an increasing feeling for simple geometrical forms. The granite pillars of the Valley Temple of Chephren followed the copies of monuments in brick and wood and the complex elegance of the group of buildings constructed for Zoser. Thus the true form of pyramid may be seen to be a geometrical simplification of the step pyramid. There is, undoubtedly, much to be said for this explanation, but it has the disadvantage of being a statement rather than an explanation and of not wholly corresponding with the conscious intentions of the ancient Egyptians. The change of shape was almost certainly brought about, or at least accompanied, by a modification of the symbolic significance of the pyramid. In an attempt to grasp this significance, we may take as our starting point some of the images included in the texts inscribed in the pyramids from the late Fifth Dynasty onwards. They are a mingling of ritual formulae and magic incantations destined to help the dead

Pharaoh to overcome the obstacles separating him from his glorious destiny, union with the sun, which would make him king for eternity. In them we may read that the Pharaoh mounted to heaven either by means of a staircase-ladder, or on a ray of the sun, two images which have long been associated with the pyramids. We have already come across the sacred stone at the sanctuary at Heliopolis: this was more or less pointed in shape, associated with the cult of the sun, and sometimes supposed to be one of its rays turned to stone. It is generally agreed that it was connected with the obelisks and the pyramids, and this is especially confirmed by the fact that, during the Sixth Dynasty, monuments similar in shape to the royal pyramids were erected at Heliopolis. By combining these elements, we may arrive at one or more hypothetical reconstructions of their formal evolution. We may suppose that the step pyramids originated from two distinct wishes; to exalt the divine nature of the Pharaoh far above his subjects by a monument pointing heavenwards, and to provide the sovereign's soul with a powerful symbolic aid in the form of a gigantic staircase in its ascension to the sun. This shape was then made similar to the stone at Heliopolis, resulting in a bent pyramid. The double slope of this type of pyramid has been frequently debated. Some hold that it is due to purely technical considerations. The builders would have preferred to erect a monument with a single slope, but prudence caused them to modify the project with the aim of reducing the weight of the upper portion and hastening its completion; the masonry at the top is clearly more hurriedly executed than at the foot. Others, however, consider that the double slope represents the wish to build a double tomb for the Pharaoh in his simultaneous capacity as King of Upper and Lower Egypt, thus expressing the dual nature of the country and its ruler.

This theory has three points against it.

First its somewhat abstract nature: symbols usually had a more practical goal than the expression of an abstract idea. Secondly, there are the two pyramids, North and South, at Dahshur which are often regarded as the northern and southern tombs; and, finally, at the side of each pyramid, there is a small satellite which some hold to be the southern tomb. Here, then, are three equally convincing solutions for a double royal burial. My own view is that the primary aim of the builders was a bent pyramid whose shape was to add to the staircase effect of the monuments preceding the stone at Heliopolis which must, in fact, have resembled this type of pyramid more than the later ones. The obelisks of the Old Kingdom were more stunted than those of later periods (for representations of the sacred stone certainly exist), and, in the sun temples of the Fifth Dynasty, there were huge obelisks with inclined pedestals, resembling the bent type of pyramid in slimmer form. These three types of monuments all have the same double slope: only the proportions are different. In my opinion, there is confirmation of the original wish to build a double slope in the shape of the copings of the walls of the lower temple and the approach road: instead of being rounded as at Giza, they are set slantways, thus harmonizing with the double slope of the pyramid.

Afterwards, still in the reign of Sneferu, the architects made a further modification which resulted in a pure pyramid. In addition to the staircase and the sacred stone, this evoked the sun's rays which sometimes pierce the clouds in a real pyramid of light by means of which the Pharaoh could rise heavenwards.

## Symbolism and temple plans

So far we have only briefly touched on the question of planning as represented by the arrangement and relationship of the various rooms. In this case, the symbols, which predominated in the selection of forms and the organization of interior masses, yielded to liturgical and theological demands. Each act of the cult took place at a predetermined point in the temple, and, conversely, every room and door formed the setting for one or more fixed phases of a ritual which, in the temples of the Late Period, was to a large extent carved on the walls of the room or on the doorposts. In every sanctuary, the Pharaoh was represented performing the essential rites due to the divinity; in the treasuries, the precious objects in store were often listed or depicted, and, in the great halls and courtyards, the processions were recorded for eternity. The arrangement and interconnection of the sanctuaries were fixed in accordance with theology which could thus distinguish the relationship of the god worshipped in one of the chapels with the others. The situation of the room helped to express the place of the god in the world of mythology. Indeed, the temple had a theoretical orientation which, in some cases, was completely different from the real one.

## Degree of freedom accorded to architects

From this we can see that the architects had a program imposed on them by the theologians. They could also be deprived of the scanty freedom remaining to them by an adherence to tradition. Almost every temple was built on the site of an ancient sanctuary either in ruins or deemed insufficient. From the ancient temple the new one inherited part of the ritual and mythological cycle on which the symbolic program had to be based. Several texts, dating from the Late Period, are explicit on this point. The part of the architect was limited, therefore, to making this program as effective as possible by means of the beauty of the building's proportions. Such a theory, however, renders us liable to misunderstand both the nature of Egyptian theology and the architect's place in society. In medieval Europe, the architect was a layman socially far below his customary employers, and without any special knowledge of theology; he could only discuss the technical aspects of the program imposed on him. In Egypt, however, the foundation of a temple implied not only building it but deciding the entire way of life depending on it. It was necessary to establish its material life by gifts of land, slaves, cattle, and valuable objects; to choose the priests and settle their hierarchy and their form of religious life; to fix the liturgy, the details of the daily ritual, the nature of the special offerings made to each god, the precise ordering of their festivals and their food. From this followed decisions regarding the theological and mythological program due to serve as a base for the temple's religious life: choosing from the many royal and regional divinities those whose support would be most effective, the connections between them to be reflected in the ritual, the exploits and attributes whose evocation would be most fit to develop their divine energy. Such was the program serving as a point of departure for the elaboration of the plan and the definition of the symbols that were to bring the architecture to life.

Painters, sculptors and masons may have been on the same social level as their medieval colleagues, but the position of architects was quite different. Apart from a number of constructional engineers, they were selected from the upper levels of various administrative branches taking part in the works and those who had the main responsibility for the building of the principal temples were usually some of the most important people in the realm. Imhotep, who built the group of funerary temples for Zoser, was chancellor to the King and was worshipped as a god in the Late Period. So was Amenhotep, son of Hapu, who was probably responsible for the Colossi of Memnon. The architects whose tombs surround the great pyramids, include a large number of princes and viziers. Inene, who built the tomb of Tuthmosis I and the fourth and fifth pylons at Karnak in the New Kingdom, was governor of Thebes and overseer of the granaries of Amon. Hapu-seneb who probably built the tomb of Tuthmosis II was high priest of Amon, and Senmut, the architect of Deir el Bahari, was overseer of the domains of Amon and tutor to the Queen's children. We have already noted that religious life could barely be distinguished from civil life at this period; it was a national concern regarding which all the chief counselors of the Pharaoh had to be consulted. In the Late Period, however, theology became the preserve of the temples, the administrative classes and the priests split up, and the social position of architects changed; from now on most of them were members of the priesthood. Thus, in every period, they belonged to the class most fitted to collaborate in the establishment of the liturgical and theological programs we have just discussed.

From this it is possible to understand that temple building did not consist of dedicating artistic and technical ability to the service of a program decided externally; it was a simultaneous theological and architectural creation.

The feeling for tradition, explicitly confirmed in texts, only partially restricted these creative acts. There are, however, other texts which bear witness to a desire to be original and indicate an anxiety not to be satisfied with tradition. Here is Amenhotep, son of Hapu, a contemporary of Amenhotep III: 'My master named me overseer of various works; I have established the king's name for eternity, I have not imitated what has been done formerly, I have created for him a mountain of quartzite . . . nobody else had done this since the ordering of the world'. It seems this was no idle boast. Inene also says: 'I alone presided over the digging of His Majesty's tomb, without sight or hearing . . . I have devised in clay plastering to decorate the tombs of their necropolis; this was something that had never

been done before since the time of creation . . . I shall be praised many years afterwards by those who copy what I have done.'

The imaginative stimulus provoked by theology, liturgy, form and technique varied according to the period and also according to the personal influence of architects such as Imhotep at Saqqara, Senmut at Deir el Bahari, and Amenhotep, son of Hapu. Creative periods were followed by others of stagnation or imitation. This will become more apparent when we study formal evolution in the last chapter and technique in Chapter III; the evolution of temple plans provides us with a particularly good illustration.

## Evolution of plans

Careful comparison of the plans included in this book will be enough to reveal their differences. Let us consider a series of temples which fall into groups because they belong to the same period and have similar dedications. First, the three temples of Lower Egypt reproduced in this book. There are only minor differences between the plans of those at Edfu and Denderah. Each has a courtyard whose axis is prolonged by four large halls, and a sanctuary completely surrounded by a corridor off which opens a series of secondary shrines. Each of the great halls plays the same part in both temples and has the same name: outer hall, often known as the pronaos, festival hall or hall of the apparition, hall of the offerings, and middle hall or hall of the ennead. The secondary shrines are arranged in identical fashion, but may be attributed to different divinities, thus reflecting local variations in mythology. At Kom Ombo, however, there are notable differences as well as many points in common. This temple is surrounded by an additional 'envelope' and its orientation is in reverse to those at Edfu and Denderah; for it is situated on the opposite bank of the Nile which is sometimes held to be a geographical axis. The rooms which were on the left are here on the right and vice versa. The most striking feature of all is the twofold sanctuary, entailing a double axis and a double series of doors. This is related to the simultaneous worship of two divinities, Horus and the crocodile god, Sebek. We know that the New Kingdom temple built approximately on the same site was dedicated to Sebek alone. An important theological change resulted in the adoption of this skilful modification of plan by which each of the gods could have the benefit of the whole forward part of the temple for his cult; all that had to be done was to close the door of his neighbor's sanctuary. Apart from the orientation and the twofold sanctuaries, the arrangement of the rooms is the same.

From this we may conclude that, in the Ptolemaic and Roman periods, important regional differences of mythological tradition resulted in secondary modifications of plan. A schematic type of temple made its appearance between the late New Kingdom and the accession of the first Ptolemies. There was still an abundance of theological invention, but the formal creative faculty was limited. We may gain a clearer

Plan of the funerary temple of Tuthmosis II

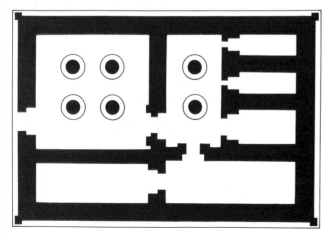

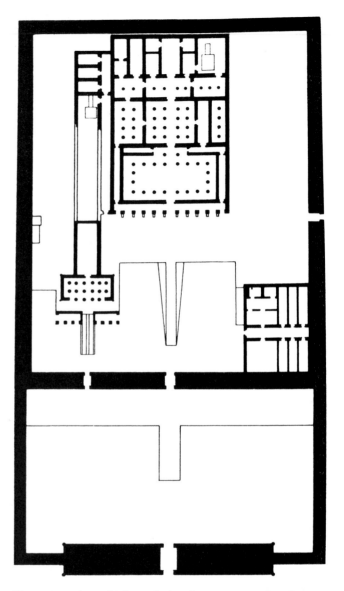

Reconstruction of plan of the funerary temple of Tuthmosis III

impression of this by following the development of the plans of the Birth Houses which formed annexes to the great temples of the Late Period. Between the Thirtieth Dynasty and the Roman Period these changed from merely temporary

98

resting places to small-scale temples; from being the scene of a humble episode in some of the great festivals, they graduated to a daily service very little different from that celebrated in the main temple.

An examination of the funerary temple of Hatshepsut at Deir el Bahari, on the other hand, will lead us to entirely different conclusions. Unfortunately, there are few available points of comparison, but we may make use of the plans of the two funerary temples that preceded and followed it: those of Tuthmosis II and Tuthmosis III. These temples are completely ruined and it has been possible only to make an approximate reconstruction of them. In the case of that of Tuthmosis II, it is scarcely possible to come to any conclusions regarding the significance of the various rooms, but a glance is sufficient to show that, architecturally, this chapel, 40 feet wide, has very little in common with the Queen's

Funerary temple of Userkaf

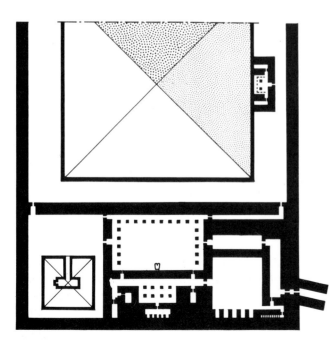

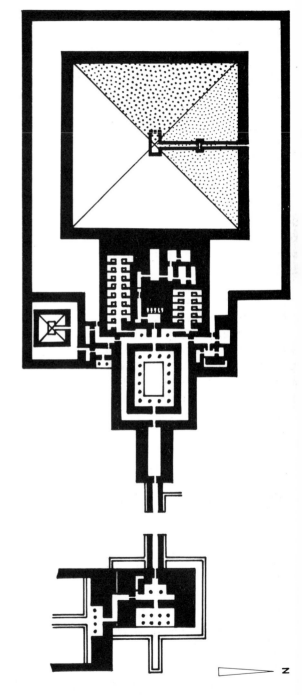

Funerary temple of Sahura

vast building. The temple of Tuthmosis III, however, was clearly inspired by that of his hated aunt. Here is the same arrangement of the staircase, the double courtyard and, on the upper level, a sanctuary dedicated to Hathor on the left and the main part of the temple in the center, which originally consisted either of a colonnaded courtyard or a hypostyle hall. Finally, after a few halls for which there is no equivalent, comes the main sanctuary, flanked on the right by a courtyard dedicated to Ra, the sun god, and, on the left, by halls of offering for the dead king and his father. Almost all these features are found in more or less identical positions, but the temple of Tuthmosis III, apart from its terraced arrangement which reproduces Deir el Bahari on a small scale, introduces them into an almost rectangular plan, similar to the majority of Egyptian temples. Thus, two fundamental principles of royal theology end in completely different architectural results. The architectural genius of Senmut took a partly new conception of the funerary temple and strove to integrate it with the landscape for theological reasons. He broke the usual rectangle of the Egyptian temple, transformed the courtyards into terraces, moved the shrines and put them in line with the colonnades, buried chapels in the rock, and made the retaining wall holding back the crumbling debris to the right of the second courtyard, into a portico.

With regard to the funerary temples adjoining the pyramids of the Old Kingdom, the dearth of contemporary texts prevents us from establishing the exact relationship between religious changes and modifications of plan. Probably there was a simultaneous effort progressively to adapt the architecture to the royal theology and a very swift change in this same theology. Ricke has put forward an exact reconstruction of this process which is still very hypothetical, but shows a profound knowledge of the nature of Egyptian architecture. A quick examination of the plans reproduced on the preceding page will reveal the extraordinary process of development that resulted, at the beginning of the Fifth Dynasty, in a solution that was maintained, with a few variations of detail, throughout the remainder of the Old Kingdom. Abandoned by Mentuhotep in the Eleventh Dynasty, it was again taken up in the early Twelfth Dynasty. The period of investigation and incessant change in this province exactly corresponded with one of continuous changes in the technical sphere.

# Plates

## Temple of Sety I at Abydos

105 Transverse aisle of the second hypostyle hall. The door at the rear was normally closed. This hall is one of the few great ones of the Ramesside period sufficiently well preserved to enable partial restoration to be made.

106 The sanctuary of Amon. The ceiling is made of horizontal, grooved slabs and the walls are decorated with representations of the cult. The upper sections are reconstructions.

107 Relief ornamenting the second hall. It is a good example of non-liturgical temple decoration and represents four goddesses paying homage to Osiris. On the left, his mother, Isis, and the goddess of the necropolis. On the right, the goddess Maat representing cosmic order, and the goddess of the years. They symbolize the benefits gained by Sety, the Osiris-king, from his funerary temple: a happy destiny after death, a permanent cosmic order, and long life here below.

## The Ramesseum at Thebes

108 One of the storehouses attached to the temple. The first courses of the brick vault are set to form small slanting arches.

109 Ruins of the first hypostyle hall.

110 Scene ornamenting the second pylon: rout of Hittite soldiers.

111 Ruins of the hypostyle hall.

## Obelisks of Karnak

112 Obelisk of Hatshepsut. The decoration consists of a series of pictures pertaining to her cult. a) A vertical text citing the titles of the queen. b) A horizontal text glorifying the queen. c) The upper part of the monument was probably faced with gold.

113 The obelisk of Tuthmosis I. The original decoration consisted of a single column of text citing the titles of the king on the center of each face. Ramesses IV added the columns on each side on his own account.

## The two temples of Abu Simbel

114 Queen Nefertari depicted at the feet of her husband.

115 General view of the site.

116 Right-hand section of the façade of the great temple. Both statues are about 65 feet high. At the king's feet are depicted various members of his family on a relatively small scale. (See plate 114.)

117 The first inner hall. The ceiling is decorated with large, hovering vultures and is supported by pillars on to which back statues of the king bearing the attributes of the god Osiris.

118- Façade of the small temple: the statues represent
119 Ramesses II and his wife Nefertari and are about 33 feet high.

## Temple of Medinet Habu

120 Monumental gateway on the east side of the fortified enclosure, based on the plan of Syrian fortresses and probably on those of contemporary Egypt as well.

121 Looking along the axis of the main part of the temple from the first pylon to the back.

122- North front of the temple. The smooth stones above
123 the door at the foot of the first pylon mark the original point of junction with the first enclosing wall, now destroyed.

124 South portico of the first courtyard.

125 West portico of the second courtyard.

## Royal Tombs

126 First section of the **Tomb of Ramesses IX.**

127 Central hall of the **Tomb of Ramesses VI.**

128 End hall of the tomb of Ramesses VI. In the foreground, the remains of the outer sarcophagus. The walls, like those of the rest of the tomb, are decorated with mysterious scenes illustrating and explaining the destiny of the king in the other world.

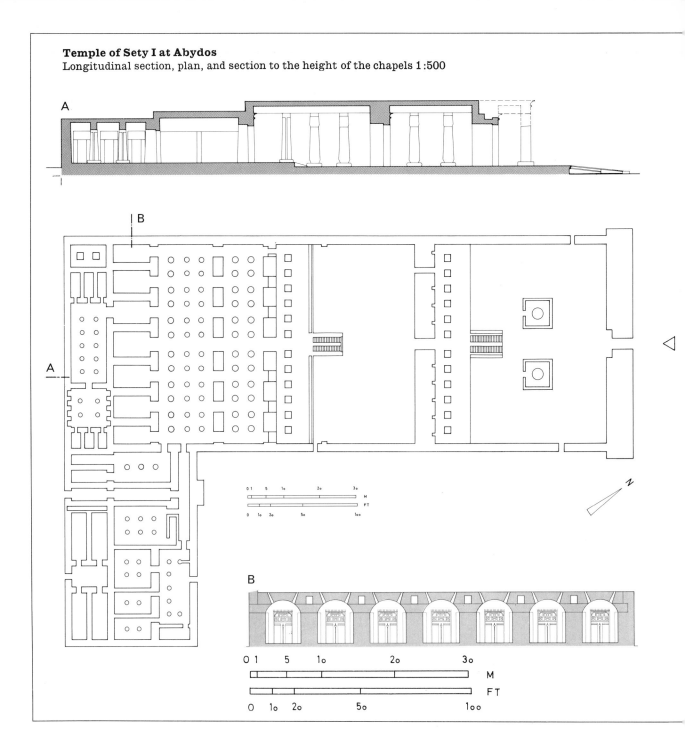

**Temple of Sety I at Abydos**
Longitudinal section, plan, and section to the height of the chapels 1:500

A

B

A

B

0 1    5    1o         2o        3o
                                        M
                                        FT
0   1o  2o        5o              1oo

0 1      5     1o              2o              3o
                                                      M

                                                      F T

0    1o  2o              5o                    1oo

## Ramesseum at Thebes
Comprehensive plan of the funerary temple and storehouses 1:2,000

## Great rock tomb of Ramesses II at Abu Simbel
Plan and longitudinal section 1:1,000

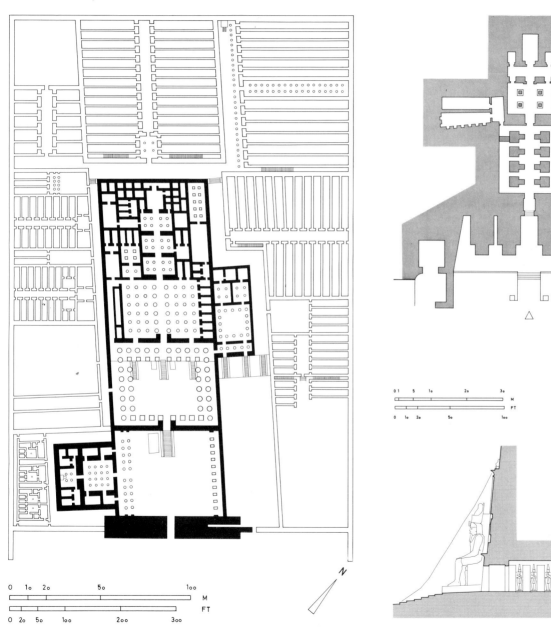

0  1o  2o        5o              1oo
M
FT
0  2o  5o    1oo        2oo        3oo

0 1  5    1o        2o        3o
M
FT
0   1o  2o      5o              1oo

N

# Notes

## Temple of Sety I at Abydos

Nineteenth Dynasty (c.1300). From a theological point of view this temple is very similar to the funerary temples, but the fact that it was dedicated to seven great gods resulted in its being given a highly unusual plan. The back of the building is occupied by a group of shrines dedicated to Osiris, the chief divinity of the region. The entire width of the building in front of this complex is taken up by a series of seven sanctuaries towards which seven axes formed by doors and widened aisles are directed across the two great pillared halls. The rooms, which in most temples are set to right and left of the chief halls, are here grouped in a wing built at right angles to the main building. The whole of this roofed part of the temple is exceptionally well preserved for a building dating from the New Kingdom. The slabs of the ceiling are often still in position and in some of the shrines the colors are unblemished. The rear portion consisting of two courts and two pylons built by Ramesses II, son of Sety I, is in a ruinous condition.

## The Ramesseum at Thebes

Nineteenth Dynasty (c.1250). This is the funerary temple of Ramesses II. The temple itself is very ruined, the rooms at the back completely destroyed, and more than half of the courtyards and the two pylons has disappeared. Almost the only features still standing are the center aisles of the first three pillared halls. Oddly enough, portions of the workshops, store-rooms and administrative buildings, constructed in rough brick, have worn better than the stone temple and constitute one of the finest examples of Egyptian civil architecture.

## Obelisks of Karnak

Eighteenth Dynasty. These obelisks are great granite monoliths which the kings of the Middle and New Kingdoms set up in pairs at the entrances to some of their temples. Those reproduced here were erected in the great temple of Karnak by Tuthmosis I and Hatshepsut. The obelisk of Tuthmosis I (c.1525) is 75 feet high, that of Hatshepsut (c.1500) nearly 100 feet high.

## Temples of Abu Simbel

Nineteenth Dynasty (c.1250). These two temples were consecrated by Ramesses II and are almost entirely hollowed out of the limestone cliff. The larger one is dedicated to the king and the chief gods of his realm: it is a translation into cliff architecture of the open air temples whose basic features may be found here in adapted forms. The pylon, usually preceded by colossal statues of the king, is recalled by the façade bounded by a rounded corner molding and an upper cornice surmounted by a frieze of monkeys which were supposed to greet the rising sun with their cries. The statues are carved in the solid rock but are not exceptional in scale. The first of the inner rooms represents the courtyard. The section usually under cover is reduced to essentials: a hypostyle hall, an antechamber, a main sanctuary and two small secondary sanctuaries. Only the storerooms and treasuries which are extended at the sides are more or less normally planned. The smaller temple is dedicated to the king's wife, Nefertari, and to the goddess Hathor. It fulfils similar functions, although on a more reduced scale.

## Temple of Medinet Habu

Twentieth Dynasty (c.1175). This is the funerary temple of Ramesses III. It is similar in plan to the Ramesseum but is in much better condition; the whole of the front portion of the actual temple-pylons and courtyards is in an excellent state of preservation. The interior has suffered more; the central area with the hypostyle halls and main sanctuaries is largely destroyed, but the flanking halls are almost intact. The usual brick enclosing wall is duplicated by an impressive system of fortifications borrowed from military usage. They are composed of a low brick wall faced with stone and a vast brick wall more than 30 feet thick and 60 feet high; on the east and west sides this is pierced by stone gates with towers.

## Tombs of Ramesses VI and Ramesses IX

Twentieth Dynasty. These Royal tombs are situated in the Valley of the Kings. They are made up of long, mainly straight, descending corridors; these sometimes widen into rooms or are interrupted by staircases and end in a large hall where the body of the sovereign was laid out in a sarcophagus. The entrance to the tomb was walled up after the burial.

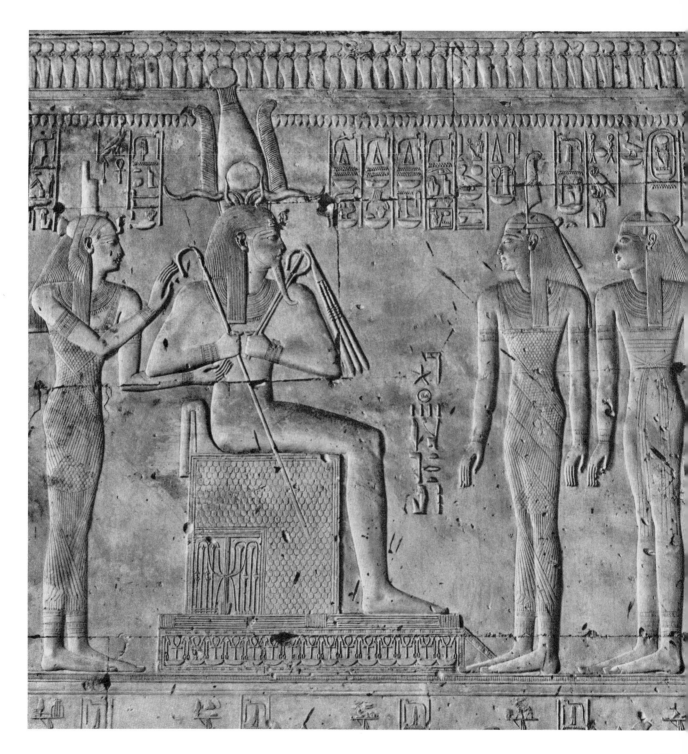

114

116

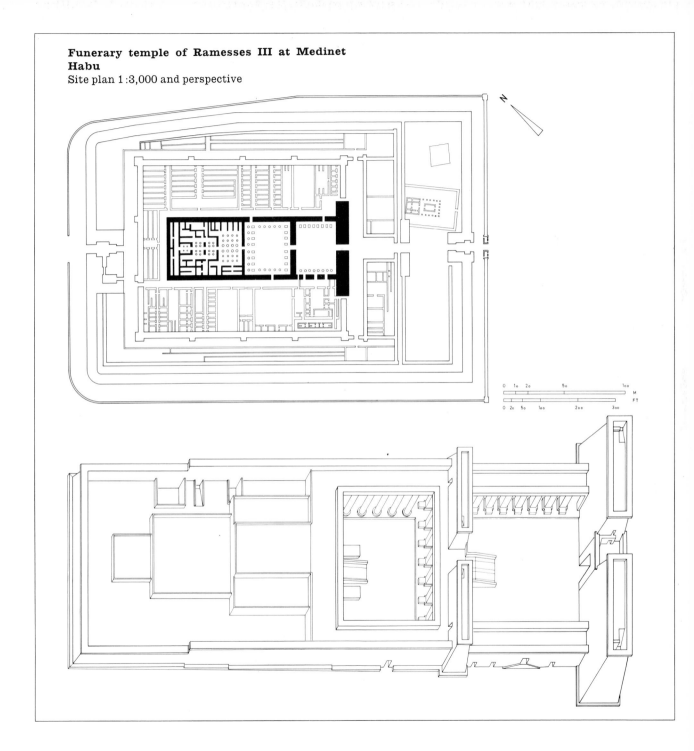

**Funerary temple of Ramesses III at Medinet Habu**
Site plan 1:3,000 and perspective

N

| 0 | 1o | 2o | 5o | 1oo | |
|---|----|-----|-----|------|---|
| | | | | | M |
| | | | | | FT |
| 0 | 2o | 5o | 1oo | 2oo | 3oo |

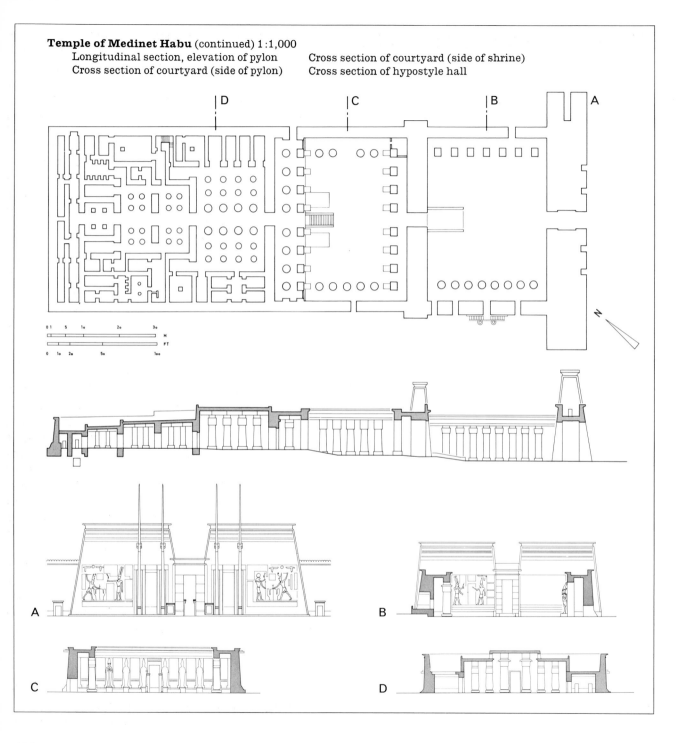

**Temple of Medinet Habu** (continued) 1:1,000
Longitudinal section, elevation of pylon     Cross section of courtyard (side of shrine)
Cross section of courtyard (side of pylon)     Cross section of hypostyle hall

# 3. Technical Problems

The Egyptian builders considered the problems of organization of work, economy, and speedy construction to be of greater importance than questions of mechanics and technical progress, the use of tough materials or more effective tools, or a quest for a more lasting, lighter form of structure. After a period of tentative investigation continuing almost until the end of the Fourth Dynasty, the principles of building construction seem to have been finally clarified and, throughout the New Kingdom, there was no clear sign of any technical change or progress. We must wait till the Twenty-fifth and Twenty-sixth Dynasties and, later still, until the Ptolemaic Period, for innovations; these included arched vaults, attempted between the Twenty-fifth and Twenty-sixth Dynasties, but used only in exceptional cases, and improved methods of preparing foundations and stone-work.

## The building of pyramids

At the beginning of the Old Kingdom, the Egyptians, who were experienced in building only with brick and timber, were faced with new and exceptionally difficult problems: the building of a pyramid is far more complex than the construction of a temple. At first sight, it may appear easy to pile up stones into a great, smooth, pointed heap, but, in fact, it demands an extraordinary degree of precision. If the result is to be a real pyramid, it is essential to ensure that every course is perfectly horizontal and that the walls are completely regular and smooth. The determination of a base more than 220 yards square is a highly complex topographical problem, especially when it has to remain convex; it would have been too costly to make the center level and then replace the stones.

The pyramids of the Old Kingdom as a rule have their four faces orientated to the four cardinal points of the compass. Here are the errors of orientation of the various faces it has been possible to check: the Pyramid of Zoser is 3° out, and that of his successor Sekhem-khet 11°—this uncompleted pyramid, conceived on the pattern of Zoser's, was discovered in 1954. At Medum, the error is no more than 24′ 25″, and at the Bent Pyramid at Dahshur about 10′; but the highest degree of accuracy is to be found at the Great Pyramid of Cheops where there is an error of 5′ 30″ for the east face and 1′ 57″ for the south. The Pyramid of Chephren shows a miscalculation of 5′ 32″ and that of Mycerinus 14′ 3″. The architects of the Fourth Dynasty were able to work out and maintain orientations over distances of about 200 yards with errors of hardly more than 10′. They obtained similar precision with horizontal surfaces: between a point at the base of the Great Pyramid near the north-west corner and another at the south-east corner, there is a difference in level of less than three-quarters of an inch. As for length, the difference between the shortest and the longest side of the Great Pyramid is less than eight inches, and the line of projection from summit to base falls less than a foot from the center of the latter, although this cannot be precisely determined as the last courses have disappeared. The means by which they arrived at these precise calculations are not known. Horizontal surfaces should not have been a great problem to people used to irrigation and must have been calculated by covering all or part of the surfaces with water. Orientations must have been worked out by taking lines on the stars, but the exact procedure is unknown. With their rudimentary methods, a minimum error of 10′ was to be expected in the projection of a sight-line on the ground. The best method proposed to date is probably the calculation of the line of bisection of an angle from the direction of the setting and rising of a circumpolar star above an artificial horizon.

The building of the pyramids raises further difficult technical problems including the cheapest method of consolidation, the resistance of the inner rooms to the vast mass surmounting them, and the rational determination of the outer shapes. The way in which these problems were resolved shows that the ancient Egyptians devoted considerable thought to the behavior of materials, the most economic and durable methods of masonry construction and to geometrical calculations.

The Egyptians were never satisfied with setting identical courses of horizontal blocks one above the other, probably because they were afraid of local subsidences. Economy forced them to make as much use as possible of the mediocre limestone of the region; the crudely–cut blocks were very cursorily matched and cemented with clay. Carefully-dressed masonry of fine limestone was kept for essential purposes and, primarily, for the facing. They seem to have thought that a central mass wholly composed of rough blocks set horizontally would not have provided the necessary cohesion; to ensure this, they adopted a succession of methods.

The Step Pyramid of Zoser is constructed round an earlier flat massif formed of horizontal blocks of masonry; this does not seem to have originally been conceived as the basis of a pyramid. The pyramid itself is composed of stones set slantways at right angles to the faces. In this way, all the blocks, including those of the facing but not those on the landings or the summit, form simple sloping rectangles. The slight gain in work was largely canceled out by the difficulty of transporting all the blocks and setting them in position. In this way the thrusts were directed towards the center line of the monument: any eventual breaking up would tend to fill up its own gaps by shifting the materials towards the interior. This type of construction was maintained for step pyramids throughout the Third Dynasty and then gradu-

Sketch of a section of the Pyramid of Sahura

ally abandoned in the reign of Sneferu who had three pyramids built. The first of these, the South Pyramid of Dahshur, known as the Bent Pyramid, is formed of horizontal blocks of masonry overlaid with a gently-inclined facing (the best preserved of all the pyramid facings in Egypt). His second monument at Medum is conceived within as a step pyramid, but the steps have been covered with a smooth facing set in horizontal courses. The last pyramid, Dahshur North, is entirely composed of horizontal blocks of masonry. If we take them in the order which seems to me to be the most likely—Dahshur South, Medum, Dahshur North—we may conclude that, after an unfortunate attempt to use horizontal blocks of masonry which was not extended to the facing where the slightest shifting would have been visible, Sneferu's architects returned to the old procedure. Later, when they were more sure of their foundations and techniques, they may possibly have again risked the more economical system of horizontal construction which was then adopted in all the other pyramids of the Old Kingdom.

Where it has been possible to study interior construction, it has been established that it does not form a homogeneous mass, but resembles the skin of an onion. A central core of crude limestone was covered with a slab of fine masonry, then with another of rough masonry and so on, until the final facing. There have been several explanations for this so-called onion construction, but the only one that appears satisfactory to me is the desire to diminish the effect of local dislocations in the rough masonry by means of the carefully dressed slabs.

A renewed search for more economical methods in the Middle Kingdom led to the adoption of

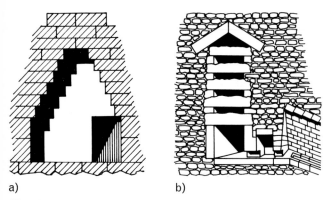

Sketch of a section of the Pyramid of Sahura: (a) Diagram of a corbel vault; (b) Section of the relieving chambers above the King's Chamber in the Pyramid of Cheops

other formulae, but these now appear to have had less lasting results as all the pyramids of this period are in a sorry state. The onion form of construction was replaced by a system of vertical walls of fine masonry set at an angle to one another along the diagonals. These walls formed the skeleton of the pyramid; the rest was made up of a rough filling of stones, rubble or bricks, the whole covered with a layer of fine limestone.

Numerous solutions were also proposed to the

problem of the resistance of the inner apartments to external pressure. In the case of the Pyramid of Zoser, these are underground and no precautions, such as horizontal ceilings hewn from the rock, have been taken, except in the first entrance corridor and the vault at the foot of the central shaft, where slabs set edgeways have been sufficient, as the space to be covered is scarcely more than five feet wide. When corridors and vaults were arranged within the actual masonry, a ceiling of plain, horizontal

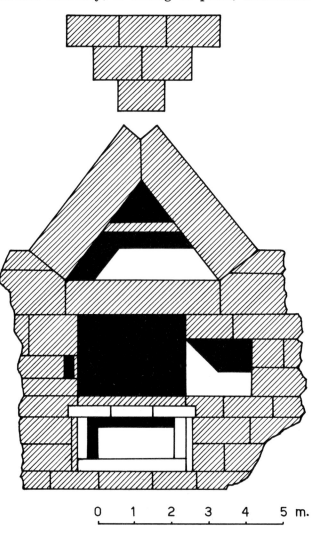

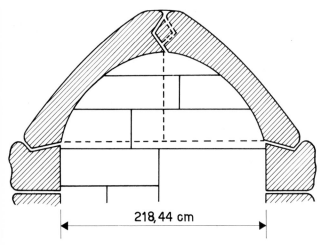

Two Middle Kingdom solutions for the erection of inverted V vaults

218,44 cm

0  1  2  3  4  5 m.

slabs was out of the question, except over very narrow spans. Sneferu gave his underground apartments very lofty corbeled vaults; each slab projects only a few inches over the one below it, so that the weight is thus spread over several elements. The lower vault of the Bent Pyramid is 96 feet wide. Cheops used the same method in his great gallery, but, later, the usual system was to roof the rooms with two slabs set in an inverted 'V'. Very often several pairs of slabs

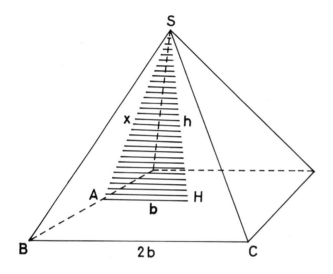

The slope of the faces is defined as h/b by modern architects

of ever-increasing dimensions were super-imposed. When the Egyptians still wished to construct a horizontal ceiling, they used what is termed a relieving arch: the slab forming the ceiling was surmounted by two blocks forming an inverted 'V' which rested either beyond the slab or on the part of it supported from below. In this way it had to carry only its own weight.

It seems clear that the slopes of the pyramids were not arbitrarily determined for their aesthetic appearance, but as a result of particular geometrical criteria, and investigations into ratios between their parts: height, edges, base,

and so on. It is difficult to be sure about this, for we have to take into account working errors made by the Egyptians and others unfortunately produced in the course of modern surveys, which are difficult to carry out when the facing is only partially preserved, as is usually the case. To arrive at these simple ratios, it is always necessary to suggest corrections which make for doubtful conclusions. The architect, J.-Ph. Lauer, has made an exhaustive study of these ratios, resulting in the following details:

**Pyramid of Zoser:** Projections: theoretical face angle: $16°$ (correction about $3'$); slope of the faces defined by the relationship of the height to half the base, i.e., the tangent of the base angle, $\dfrac{7}{2} = \dfrac{1 \text{ cubit}}{2 \text{ palms}}$

**Bent Pyramid:** (a) Lower section: angle of the edge with the base plane: $45°$ (correction $13'$ $45''$); slope $\dfrac{7}{5} = \dfrac{1 \text{ cubit}}{5 \text{ palms}}$; (b) Upper section: slope of the edge $\dfrac{2}{3}$ (correction $2'$); slope of the faces $\dfrac{17}{18} = \dfrac{1 \text{ cubit 6 fingers' breadth}}{1 \text{ cubit 8 fingers' breadth}}$.

**North Pyramid, Dahshur:** as for the upper section of the Bent Pyramid.

**Pyramid of Medum:** theoretical angle $51° 50'$; slope of the face $\dfrac{14}{11} = \dfrac{1 \text{ cubit}}{5 \text{ palms 2 fingers' breadth}}$; slope of the edge: $\dfrac{9}{10}$ (correction $4''$).

**Pyramid of Cheops:** same as above.

**Pyramid of Chephren:** slope of the face $\dfrac{4}{3}$ (height and base of the so-called sacred triangle with sides 3, 4, 5).

The ratio of the median of one of the faces to half the base equals the golden number 1.618.

**Pyramid of Mycerinus:** theoretical angle 51° 20′ 25″ (correction 2′ 12″); slope of face

$$\frac{5}{4} = \frac{\text{1 cubit 7 fingers' breadths}}{\text{1 cubit}}.$$

**Pyramid of Unas:** theoretical angle: 56° 19′;

$$\text{slope } \frac{3}{2} = \frac{1\frac{1}{2} \text{ cubits}}{\text{1 cubit}}.$$

From these figures Lauer concludes that the builders aimed especially at 'a slope angle easy to build and correct' and 'ratios $\frac{h}{b}$ $\left(\frac{\text{height}}{\text{half the base}}\right)$ composed of whole numbers as simple as possible'. Up to the time of Cheops their special wish was to simplify the calculation of the slope of the edge; afterwards, they concentrated on the slopes of the faces.

The mathematical texts discussed in Chapter I to some extent confirm these conclusions, but they need to be presented somewhat differently if we are to gain a better understanding of the preoccupations of the ancient Egyptians. For them, the slope was the length required for half the base when the height was equal to 1 (one cubit). So, having made the numerators of the fractions quoted by Lauer equal to one cubit, we must invert them. We must also bear in mind that they could not express a ratio such as 14/11 as, apart from 2/3, they knew nothing of any fractions that did not have 1 as the numerator. This does not mean that they could not understand the sides of a triangle for example in the ratio 3:4:5, only that they could not express this in simple mathematical symbols. (Slopes with a ratio of $\frac{\text{4 palms, 1 finger's breadth}}{\text{4 palms, 2 fingers' breadth}}$ must, therefore, have been eyed with suspicion).

In my opinion, however, the adoption of one of these simple slopes would not have specially simplified the ground work. From the moment when each workman engaged on the facing had a cubit's length where a guiding mark indicated the length defining the slope, it made very little difference to him whether this mark was placed at one or other point on his ruler. These ratios would appear to have been determined by a search for simplicity in calculation and a theoretical wish to discover enticingly easy geometrical solutions. This entirely personal opinion obviously credits the Egyptians with a greater feeling for abstract mathematics than is attributed to them by the experts.

The majority of the ratios presented by Lauer lend themselves too easily to translation into the system of Egyptian mathematical exercises for us not to see them as a confirmation. A considerable number of fractions in the above list have one cubit as a numerator. In these cases, the Egyptian slope is simply expressed by the denominator $\frac{\text{1 cubit}}{\text{5 palms, 1 finger's breadth}} =$ a slope of 5 palms, 1 finger's breadth, and this slope must have been simply expressed in the Egyptian system of units. The best confirmation lies in the slopes proposed by Lauer for the Pyramid of Sneferu at Medum and the Pyramid of Cheops: $5\frac{1}{2}$ palms; this is, in fact, the slope adopted in four out of five exercises on the pyramids inscribed on the papyrus in question.

Section through foundations of the temple at Medinet Habu

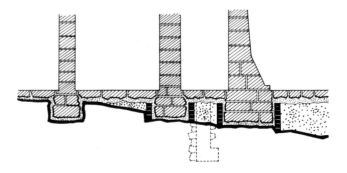

The architects were not faced with the same difficulties in the building of temples. The chief problems that had to be solved here were connected with foundations, roofing, the masonry of walls and pillars, lighting, and decoration; these merely demanded the application of simple formulae that had already been long established, and certainly did not exact the same degree of precision as the building of the pyramids.

## Foundations of temples

This is made particularly clear when we come to examine the foundations of the principal temples which often produce an impression of great carelessness. Nevertheless, as many of these buildings have survived for over three thousand years, they cannot have been so badly thought out; yet they ill accord with the widespread idea, based on the pyramids, of the technical perfection of Egyptian architecture. The general principle was to dig a trench a little wider than the wall to be supported, and to line the bottom of it with a thin covering of sand which was stopped from running away by little side walls made of brick. The real foundations were laid in this trench: stones for the main walls, bricks for the less weighty features. The empty spaces were afterwards filled up with sand. In theory this process was adequate for use in a firm soil, but in clay, the slightest infiltration could cause a subsidence.

The architects did not always take care to separate features which were liable to subside at different rates owing to their dissimilar weights. Sometimes, for instance, an average-sized wall and a pylon were firmly linked together, instead of being separated by a groove, and this considerably speeded up damage resulting from the slightest subsidence of the foundations.

These foundations obviously varied greatly in depth according to the weight they had to support and the type of soil. Those of the great brick outer wall at Medinet Habu—$34\frac{1}{2}$ feet wide and about 60 feet high—were 10 feet deep in clay soil. At Karnak the foundations of the eighth pylon, also built on clay, were nearly 10 feet deep. On firmer soil, such as the broken rock at Deir el Bahari, the depth was often quite insignificant—a layer of stones, 20 inches or less—and low brick walls were often built directly on the sand without any trench at all.

The actual foundations were often composed of seemingly inadequate materials: small stones, sometimes set edgeways below a first course of large blocks placed lengthways, or various elements taken from earlier ruined monuments. Huge squared blocks and drums or half-drums of columns were set side by side, leaving between them empty spaces unfilled by mortar. This motley collection of masonry frequently shifted ground, causing fractures in the lower courses.

From the Twenty-fifth Dynasty onwards, and especially during the Ptolemaic Period, greater care was taken with regard to foundations: the great temples of later periods were built on proper platforms formed of several layers—up to nine or ten—of well-dressed slabs.

Detail of roofing of hypostyle hall at Karnak

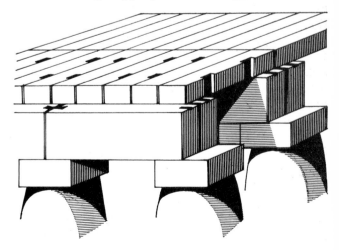

137

# Ceilings

The building of ceilings clearly called for greater care as faulty construction would have had more direct consequences. Nevertheless, a marked increase in strictness is not noticeable. In the time of the New Kingdom, ceilings consisted of a single thickness of large slabs set flat across the architraves. In the Late Period, religious ceremonies taking place on roofs seem to have become more important and a second layer of slabs or a pavement of irregular squares, carefully pointed, was frequently added. Under the Old Kingdom, the ceiling slabs were usually set edgeways and rounded to appear like wooden beams. The chief difficulty was the working out of the length and thickness of the architraves in relation to the weight of the roof and the materials employed. The length chosen determined the spacing of the columns. Apparently the architects had no well-defined set of rules. Sometimes the architraves are clearly loaded in excess of what would now be considered a safety margin, although in many cases this has not prevented their holding firm for three thousand years, and they are often thicker than need be, especially over small doors. The architects' conjectural idea of the resistance of materials is clearly revealed in the way in which they coupled the blocks of the architrave: instead of using single blocks, they often placed two side by side. This did not make a great difference to the stability of the building, but, sometimes, they topped one block with another, and this did. Above one of the monumental gateways at Karnak dating from the Thirtieth Dynasty, is a device that indicates that they sometimes grasped the difference. Here the lintel supports a very heavy entablature; to relieve it, the lower surfaces of the two blocks surmounting it are lightly hollowed out throughout its length and merely rest on the doorposts. The only notable advance that can be recorded during the New Kingdom is the replacement of limestone by

Sketch showing constructional method for arched brick vaults

sandstone, a lighter substance with greater tensile strength. Limestone allowed a span of 10 feet; with sandstone, this rose to 33 feet.

The Egyptians seldom used vaults as constructional features of their stone temples. When, probably for religious reasons, they needed concave ceilings, these were erected over fairly narrow spans and the arcading was either hewn out of the thick slabs overhead or out of a corbel vault whose steps were cut back. Thus it was more a question of a sham vault. The upper face of the ceiling remained completely flat.

In both civil and religious brick architecture, on the other hand, vaulting was the only device which made it possible to avoid the use of expensive imported timber. It was frequently used over comparatively wide spans of more than 13 feet. Large halls could be roofed by division into several vaulted aisles supported by ranges of columns. In the case of small spans this sometimes involved the use of voussoirs, but the more usual device—the only solution in the case of wide spans—was that of vaults formed of inclined courses. The curved portions of the vault were made of flat bricks with an uneven surface; these were laid slantways so that they held one another in position, thus enabling the

builders to dispense with inner frameworks of timber or fillings of earth. Vaults of this kind were supported by vertical walls the strength of which was increased by several layers of bricks—usually ten or more were used. In this case only the first thickness was set slantways, but the first two or three courses were sometimes inclined to one side or the other, resulting in a much stronger framework.

Oddly enough in a country where it very seldom rains, one of the most marked features of the roofs is their ability to keep out water. The slightest infiltration of this into the painted rooms would have caused ugly streaks on the decoration and offended the canons of religion. The usual principle was to hollow out small ducts running along the joints of the slabs which were stopped by sectional plugs in the

Drainage system for rainwater in a section of the temple at Abydos

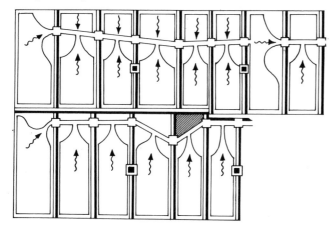

Watertight joints between two ceiling slabs (Abydos, Medinet Habu)

Various systems of light openings used in temples

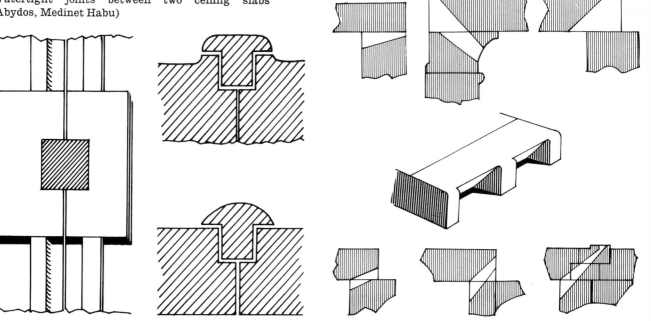

## Lighting

Light was most often introduced from the roof. The type of window at human height normally used in houses, is seldom found in temples as such windows do not allow a subtle distribution of light. In the great hypostyle halls of the Ramesside temples, however, there is a device which may be termed a window. The roofs of these halls are on two levels, the central range of columns being higher and of a different type from those at the sides. The three central aisles are loftier than the others and the projections of the tops of the second-line columns from the center are provided with stone grilles, often called clerestory windows, which direct an evenly diffused light over the axis of the hall. This device was later abandoned, probably for symbolic reasons, and there was a revival of the old system which provided a more reduced, mysterious, controlled form of lighting. The light falls regularly from above through crevices or round or square holes pierced at the tops of the walls, between the roofing slabs, or in the ceilings; these long, narrow openings provide beams of light which leave the greater part of the hall in darkness and pick out a few chosen details.

## Walls and pillars

The same mixture of exactitude, empirical approximation, and economy as was used over

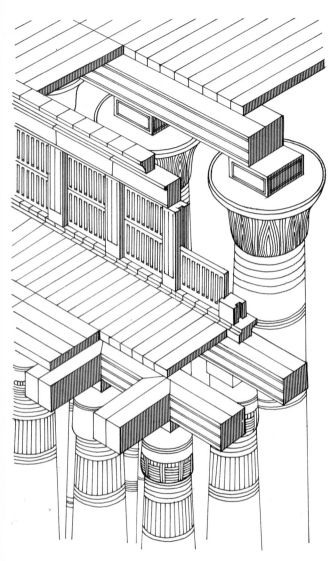

System of clerestory lighting used in the great halls of the Ramesside Period (hypostyle hall at Karnak)

shape of mushrooms. The edges of the openings arranged in the ceilings were slightly raised. The water flow was cleverly devised: in smaller buildings, the roof had a gentle, even slope guiding the water into a gutter at the side, or a complex system of sloping channels directed it into the spouts and gutters.

Masonry from Zoser's tomb complex: in contrast to later technique, the blocks join only near the surface of the wall

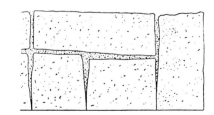
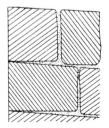

foundations and roofing can be noted in the masonry of walls and columns. Very few walls of any thickness are built as an entity. Instead, they are formed of two carefully executed faces between which there is either more gimcrack masonry or even loose rubble. This was a dangerous method for walls above a certain height. Most of the pylons at Karnak, for instance, have an outer shell no more than one block thick; the space inside is sometimes divided into compartments by highly-finished partition walls and filled up with a variety of blocks heaped together without mortar. In the case of diffuse masses as high as these, the slightest inner fall would be enough to ruin the outer envelope. The masonry of the facings, however, was very carefully executed, reaching a precision which was largely responsible for the reputation of the builders of Egypt. The amazing perfection of the outer facing of the Great Pyramid is a well-known example. Blocks often weighing over ten tons are so expertly put together that it is seldom possible to slip a needle or a piece of paper between the joins. The facings of the New Kingdom, though not so perfect, were, nevertheless, almost always of high standard. Walls were usually composed of horizontal, irregular courses. Except in the Late Period, when the blocks were hewn into a standard shape in the quarries and were almost all of the same dimensions, the stones which arrived on the sites were of very different sizes. When a course was completed, the masons were confronted with a horizontal bed of stone. The stones of the following course, chosen from those of almost equal height, were carefully smoothed first on the lower, then on the side faces, but the lines of the resulting joins were by no means necessarily vertical and at right angles to the wall. The only obvious necessity was that the two faces that had to meet should be parallel; the exact direction of the lines depended on which afforded the greater economy in stone. These operations seem to have been carried out on the ground and involved methods which have still not been precisely determined.

The blocks, with three faces still rough, were then placed on a bed which was spread with mortar in a sufficiently liquid state to ensure both the movement of the blocks after their laying in position and their future adherence to one another secured by their weight. While the mortar was drying, the blocks were linked to one another by dovetail joints of wood, stone, or metal which were often removed later. When all the stones of the course had been laid, the upper surface was leveled off to form a bed for the following course. The rear face of the blocks was left as it was and the surface of the facing was not smoothed until the wall was completed. Then it received a coating of stucco if the stone was of indifferent quality, and was then handed over to the painters and sculptors responsible for its decoration. The placing of the decoration could completely alter the character of surfaces, causing similar buildings to appear of different proportions. A pylon covered from top to bottom with a variety of scenes looked quite different from one which contrasted garishly-colored rectangles with two symmetrical scenes showing a massacre of prisoners or the gaudy friezes of its cornice with wide areas of sparkling white occupying the remainder of its surface. The difference may be noted in the case of the two obelisks reproduced in this book. That of Tuthmosis I is decorated with three regular columns of text; the obelisk of Hatshepsut has, in succession, from top to bottom, a series of scenes taking up the entire width of the face, a center column of large hieroglyphs, and a rectangle of condensed text again occupying the entire width. If we recall that the signs were painted in lively colors, that the topmost scenes were probably faced with gold, and that elsewhere the granite was left plain, it is clear that these two monuments of similar shape must have given completely different impressions.

Contractors, engineers, architects and builders had to devote their attention to a series of problems that included choice, transport and setting up of materials. Given the need for economy and the simple mechanical means available, these problems must have assumed as much importance as those relating to the actual building.

The choice of materials was naturally dictated by both economic and religious factors. Secondary temples, annexes to the main ones, such as enclosures or administrative buildings, could be built of brick which was far cheaper than stone; these bricks were merely dried in the sun as there was very little to be gained by using fired bricks in a country where both fuel and rainfall were scarce. Stone was indispensable for the main temples as it was the only material ensuring perpetuity. There was abundance of stone in Egypt, but there was also great variation in quality and price. Rough limestone was used from the neighbourhood of the site, sandstone was cheap, light, and easily transportable, but ill suited to fine carving; there were also available, fine limestone, granite, alabaster, crystalline sandstone or red quartzite, and black basalt from the Arabian mountains. Rough limestone was used for fillings, sandstone and fine limestone for the main constructional work. The other materials were reserved for the most sacred and important sections of the temple.

The next stage was to determine the most convenient shape for the blocks. Various solutions were adopted. In the complex of Zoser the stones are no more than large bricks and the courses are about 10 inches high, but in his successor's buildings the courses are already twice this height. The size of the blocks continued to increase until the reigns of Cheops and Chephren. In the Pyramids of Giza they grow steadily smaller with the rise of level showing that difficulties of transport here took precedence. The lower courses measure from 3 to $4\frac{1}{2}$ feet, those at the top from 20 to 24 inches. The blocks of the upper and lower temples of Chephren are still larger. The average volume must be slightly more than 35 cubic feet. Later it tends to decrease. At Medinet Habu, in the time of the New Kingdom, the blocks vary from 12 to 35 cubic feet, those of the architrave, of course, being larger. In the Late Period, the average size was clearly smaller.

The transport of normal-sized stones involved no special difficulties: they were hauled on runners either by men or beasts and then loaded on to barges. The conveyance of the huge single blocks required for obelisks and colossal statues, on the other hand, formed one of the most arduous tasks those in charge of the works had to face and it was this aspect of their work they were most willing to boast about, though the terms they used are too general to enable exact definition of the methods employed. It is quite likely, however, that they were dragged manually over tracks of mud and loaded on to specially constructed boats. Once on the site, they had to

Method of building a large hall using brick ramp and fillings of rubble

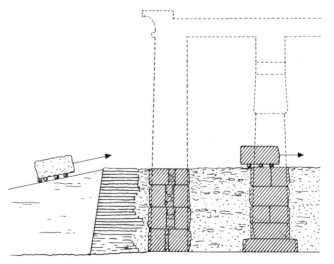

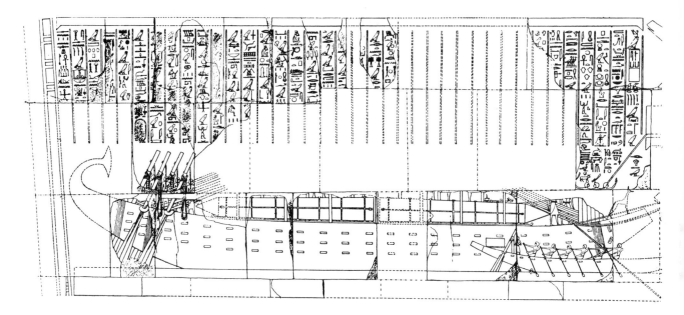

Transport of two obelisks in a barge (relief from the temple of Deir el Bahari)

be set up. Unfortunately, we have no information as to how this operation, which must have been the most difficult of all, was carried out. The supposition is that the obelisk was raised on to great heaps of sand; by piling this up towards its foot it could have been made to slide gently on to its pedestal, reaching it in a sufficiently upright position to enable the end of the operation to be carried out with the help of ropes. The success of such exceptional operations should not blind us to the fact that the basic problem was the setting in position of the more ordinary features such as the blocks of walls, pillars and ceilings. There was no particular difficulty here, although the erection of an architrave more than 30 feet long at a height of over 60 feet without the aid of pulleys can never have been an easy task.

In the case of the temples there was no question of using scaffolding which would have involved a vast quantity of very expensive timber imported from the Lebanon, even for average size blocks. Apparently the Egyptians built their great halls by filling them up gradually with bricks, mud and rubble. After laying all the blocks of the first course, they filled up the area so formed with the cheapest possible materials; then they laid the second course, filled this up, and so on. Thus, at each level they created what amounted to a platform on which the builders could operate. When they reached the summit, they set up the architrave on the tops of the columns, or rather the abaci, filled up the space with a last layer of rubble and then laid the ceiling slabs. Afterwards, they began to clear out the rubble and, as its level gradually decreased, smoothed the surfaces of walls and columns.

Light scaffolds made from local timber were then used by the decorators who applied the stucco work and carved and painted the walls. Exterior ramps were certainly used to hoist the blocks to each level: traces of some still survive. They were made of a shell of bricks filled with rubble and mud erected at right angles to the walls throughout their length. The blocks of stone were probably hoisted on to these ramps on runners.

In the building of the pyramids, the size of the stones and the height to which they had to be hoisted placed further emphasis on this side of the work; but we know less about it than in the case of the temples. Many reconstructions have been made, but there is none which explains all the facts satisfactorily. Some authorities even question the use of ramps on account of a passage in Herodotus which mentions machines used for lifting. Those who agree to the employment of ramps differ as to their number—from one to at least four—and their arrangement, whether spiral ramps or at right angles to the faces.

There is almost universal agreement that the pyramids were built up in successive horizontal sections, each course being laid over the whole area of the section before carrying on with the next one. This is a likely theory and the only one that provides a suitable working platform throughout the operation, but, unfortunately, it is difficult to apply it to pyramids built on a slant. The intervals between the few dates that have been noted on different levels of the facing of some pyramids also accord badly with this theory in that they are too close together.

Clearly, then, insurmountable difficulties present themselves at the outset of any attempt to reconstruct building methods, causing every solution to be uncertain. We shall confine ourselves to the one which appears most logical and most suited to what we know about the working methods of later periods and the organization and economic outlook of the builders of Egypt. In J.-Ph. Lauer's opinion, the pyramids were built up course by course with the aid of a

single ramp at right angles to one of the faces. This ramp was so devised that the width of its upper face decreased in proportion to the height it reached. For the amount of stones needed for each course diminished rapidly as the structure

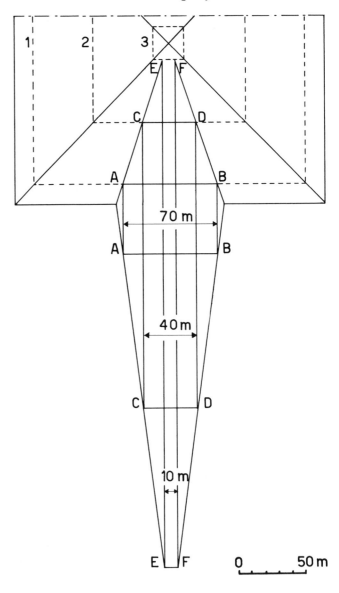

Outline of constructional ramp for a pyramid, after Lauer

rose. If a width of between 230 and 330 feet was needed at the base, eight feet would be sufficient at the top. In the case of the Great Pyramid, a ramp of this kind, with a base of 330 feet and a slope of 15°, would have had a volume of 1.3 million cubic yards, about two-fifths of the volume of the Pyramid. Finally, as in the case of the temples, it was necessary, in order to permit the arrangement of the facing blocks from a point directly opposite, to erect a shell of bricks around the pyramid, thus creating a working platform from which the blocks could be laid on the way up and the faces could be smoothed on the way down.

## Plans

The basic features of architects' plans were sketched on papyrus, but we must be very careful in judging their nature as only a few examples have survived. The only document which can be identified with any certainty as an architect's plan is the papyrus in the Museum at Turin containing a projected design for the tomb of Ramesses IV. There are differences in proportion between the design and the tomb as we know it today which indicates that the papyrus ante-dates the digging of the tomb and confirms that it represents a project and not a survey. The principle of the plan is simple: the contours of the excavation are indicated by double strokes and the chief details, such as doors, are sketched on the plan in reduced elevation. The proportions are only roughly defined and have to be deduced from written numbers indicating the length, width and height of each room. Important details, such as the thickness of the doors, are left out. A plan of this sort would not satisfy a present-day contractor, but perhaps it was enough for the Egyptian builders. The architect was identical with the contractor and could, therefore, give the necessary details to the workmen on the site. It is, however, quite likely that this plan was completed by more

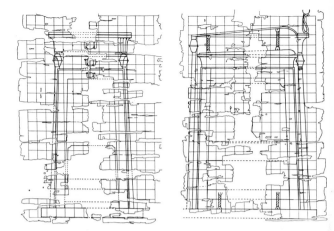

Front and side elevations of a wooden shrine, drawn on squared papyrus

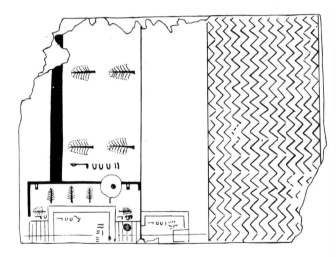

Plan of a rest pavilion

detailed diagrams. We have a few documents that could answer to this purpose, although, of course, not for this tomb. They include a sketch for a blind door on a fragment of limestone and a remarkable design for a shrine on 'squared' papyrus dating from the New Kingdom. The latter shows how exact these designs could be. It also shows that the Egyptians knew how to represent an object from several angles. The two elevations reveal a number of interior features as in a transparency and also play the part of sections. Squaring was again often used for projected wall decorations: remains of it can still frequently be seen on the walls of tombs and temples.

The conclusions drawn from this selection of documents are fully confirmed by a number of architectural sketches, usually executed on limestone fragments. One of these, more than 30 inches long, has preserved for us a project for the tomb of Ramesses IX, very similar to that shown on the Turin papyrus. There is also a tablet of wood which carries a plan, probably for a small pavilion. There are many other drawings of this type which are no more than rapid, free-hand sketches. The most valuable is one of a curve which was found in the enclosure of King Zoser at Saqqara and must, therefore, date from the Third Dynasty; the vertical lines theoretically placed at equal distances from one another and the numbers indicating their length from an unmarked horizontal level define the co-ordinates of a number of points on the curve. In this lies proof that, from this period onwards, the Egyptians had a very exact idea of graphic representation. This curve must have corres-

ponded to the roof of one of the buildings of Zoser's complex.

We cannot be sure whether plans were amplified by maquettes, though the Egyptians often executed models of buildings. Models of granaries and workshops have frequently been discovered in tombs of the First Intermediate Period and the Middle Kingdom. Many stone reproductions of sections of temples also survive, but it is uncertain whether these are really the projected designs of architects.

If there has been too great insistence in this chapter on the technical weaknesses of Egyptian building construction, it is because this aspect of their architecture is one that is most frequently ignored. It would be absurd, however, to claim that the Egyptians were bad builders. They have left monuments still standing in their defence and in some spheres, particularly during the Old Kingdom, they attained a degree of precision which it would be difficult to surpass even with modern methods of measurement and up-to-date lifting gear. The Egyptian architects and masons knew how to build well, but, especially in the time of the New Kingdom, they had to build quickly and pay great attention to the cost. When it was a question of profiting from religion, the king did not hesitate to make lavish use of precious materials or to have the hardest stone molded with a precision that still defies explanation; but, for the majority of buildings, saving in material, labor and time was the chief consideration of the builders. The foundation of a temple was linked with the person of a resolute king who wished to be able to benefit as soon as possible from the greatest possible number of temples. With the Late Period the link between the monarchy and the temples became less personal, thus contributing to less haste and improved quality of construction. Almost all the weaknesses we have examined resulted from this desire for economy.

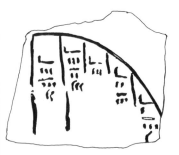

Definition of the curve of a roof by a system of coordinates (Third Dynasty)

# Plates

## Temple at Edfu

151 The western face of the pylon. The four registers of the decoration show King Ptolemy XIII making offerings to the chief divinities of the temple.

152 The southern face of the pylon. In the foreground, the remains of the section preceding the Birth House. The pylon has lost its topmost cornice. The four vertical grooves on either side of the gateway served to hold the bases of the wooden masts which rose well above the summit of the pylon. They were kept in position by means of metal claws fixed in the double series of square holes above the grooves. The lower register of the decoration shows the king dedicating his vanquished enemies to Horus, striking them with his mace.

153 View from the top of the pylon. In the background, the remains of the brick enclosure. Note the traces of dovetail joints on the summit of the wall, destined to hold the blocks in place.

154- The great vestibule or pronaos.
155

156 The main sanctuary, or holy of holies, with the shrine which enclosed the statue of the god and the pedestal on which his portable bark was placed.

157 The ambulatory surrounding the holy of holies.

158 Exterior of the main sanctuary. The openings in the ceiling form part of the original lighting system.

159 View from the main sanctuary along the axis of the temple.

## Temple at Denderah

160 Façade of the temple. In the foreground, portion of the unfinished outer wall.

161 Angle of the roof, with cornice and torus molding. Comparison with plate 158 clearly shows the difference in the detailed treatment of the same features at Edfu and Denderah: the relief shown here is more accentuated and rounded than that at Edfu.

162 Exterior of the temple, west front. Right background, the small temple dedicated to the goddess Isis.

163 Detail of the western exterior wall with a waterspout in the form of a lion. Note the blocks laid in regular courses. Slanting joints are still used, though not nearly so often as in earlier buildings.

164 Light opening in one of the chapels built on the terrace of the temple. This chapel was dedicated to the celebration of the death and resurrection of the god Osiris. The light passes over the body of the god, who is shown on his death-bed in the opening, and brings him back to life. This is a typical example of the symbolic use of a practical feature.

165 Interior of the great vestibule. The ceiling is supported by Hathor-head columns and decorated with astronomical scenes.

## Temple of Kom Ombo

166 View of the temple looking towards the entrance from the main sanctuaries. In the background is the Nile and, on the right, the ruins of the Birth House. The parts of the temple shown are the higher mass of the great vestibule, one of the columns of the second hall, and the three rooms preceding the sanctuaries. The empty space between the two partition walls separating the sanctuaries was probably a crypt, examples of which have been found within many of the walls of temples of the Late Period: they were reached by a system of secret openings and were used to store precious objects.

167 Shaft of one of the columns of the second hall.

168 Capitals of the great vestibule. These belong to the composite type: the slim shaft is interrupted, slightly below the capital, by a band from which emerge the stalks of various plants whose flowers are carved on the capital.

169 The great vestibule.

170 Unfinished relief in one of the eastern chapels, showing the technical methods used; the figures are completed but the texts have still to be carved.

## Map of the Luxor region 1:100,000

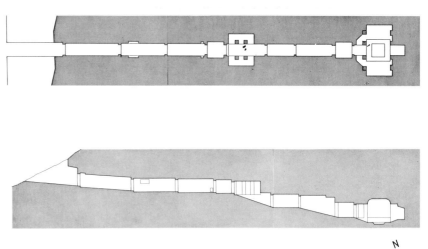

1 Town of Luxor
2 Temple of Luxor
3 Temple of Mut
4 Temple of Karnak
5 Valley and tombs of the Queens
6 Temple of Deir el Medineh
7 Temple of Medinet Habu
8 Colossi of Memnon
9 Tombs of the nobles
10 Temple of Meneptah
11 Temple of Tuthmosis IV
12 Ramesseum
13 Temple of Tuthmosis III
14 Valley and tombs of the Kings
15 Temples of Mentuhotep and Hatshepsut at Deir el Bahari
16 Temple of Sety I and Ramesses II

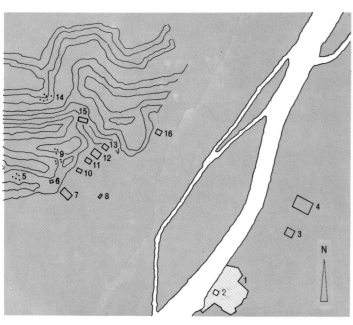

**Tomb of Ramesses VI in the Valley of the Kings**
Plan and cross section 1:1,000
**Tomb of Ramesses IX in the Valley of the Kings**
Plan 1:1,000

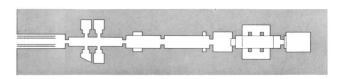

**Great temple of Horus at Edfu**
Plan and cross section 1:1,000

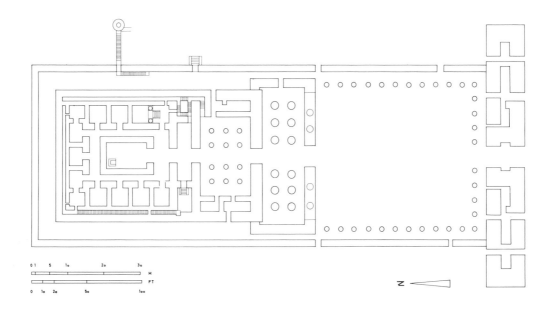

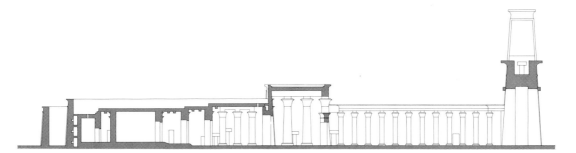

# Notes

## Temple at Edfu

This is the best preserved of all the Egyptian temples. The actual structure is more or less intact, only lacking the upper cornice of the pylon and a few scattered blocks of stone; almost all the slabs of the ceiling are in position. The paintings which must have completely covered the walls have disappeared altogether along with all the features, such as doors, made of wood or metal. Around the chief temple there are now only scanty traces of the great surrounding brick wall and a Birth House, the front portion of which is fairly ruinous: in the vestibule and pillared sanctuaries at the back, however, there are traces of the original colored decoration.

The building of the temple, like all the important complexes of the Graeco-Roman period, extended over several generations. Work began in 237 B.C. and the core of the temple—the sanctuaries and three halls preceding them in enfilade—was probably finished by 212, although the decoration continued until 147. The great vestibule, sometimes known as the first hypostyle hall or pronaos, was not completed until 122. The courtyard, pylon and outer wall were erected in the late second and early first centuries; their decoration was not completed until 57 B.C.

The plan is considered the archetype of the great buildings of the Late Period. It consists of a pylon, a pillared court whose exterior wall is prolonged round the core of the temple, a large vestibule opening on to the courtyard wider and higher than the rest of the temple, a suite of three halls in enfilade flanked by secondary chambers including the treasury and staircase, and a central sanctuary where the statue of the god was housed in a stone shrine. This sanctuary is isolated from the rest and protected by a corridor or ambulatory on to which opens a series of secondary shrines.

## Temple at Denderah

This temple was begun about the time when that at Edfu reached completion. The building of the great vestibule must have been finished during the reign of the Emperor Tiberius (14-37 A.D.), but the decoration was not completed until Nero's reign (54-68 A.D.). The other projected features, such as the pylon, the courtyard in front of the great vestibule, and the exterior wall, were abandoned almost before reaching the foundation stage. The completed section is almost as well preserved as the temple at Edfu; there are clear traces of color here and there and the shrines on the roof, which at Edfu have disappeared, still stand. The subsidiary buildings round the temple within the enclosure, bounded by a brick wall built to the order of Domitian, are better excavated than those at Edfu and it is still possible to see the sacred lake, two Birth Houses—one begun under Nectanebo I (Thirtieth Dynasty), the other dating from the Roman period—a small temple dating from the reign of Augustus dedicated to the goddess Isis, and the ruins of various brick monuments. The temple is conceived in accordance with the classic plan for the great buildings of the Late Period: a great vestibule, loftier and wider than the rest of the temple, and a succession of three large halls leading to the central sanctuary which is surrounded by a corridor on to which open the subsidiary shrines. Its chief claim to originality lies in the columns of the vestibule which represent the sistrum; this was chosen in honor of the goddess Hathor to whom the temple was dedicated.

## Temple at Kom Ombo

Owing to its poor state of preservation this temple cannot be compared with the two previous ones. The pylon, courtyard, outer walls, and most of the sanctuaries are either razed to the ground or else merely survive a few feet above it. Only the central section between the two main sanctuaries, but exclusive of them, and the great vestibule still stand. Nevertheless, the temple has a charm which contrasts with the austere beauty of Edfu: this is owing to its fine situation on the banks of the Nile and the ochre patina of the limestone of which it is built.

It was constructed in a succession of 'envelopes'. The core consisting of the sanctuaries and four halls in enfilade were the work of Ptolemy VI and Ptolemy VII (181-116 B.C.). The great vestibule, intermediate enclosure, and the sanctuaries adjoining the east front date from the first half of the first century B.C.; the court and outer wall were executed to the order of Tiberius (14-37 A.D.).

The plan is appreciably different from those of Edfu and Denderah. As the temple is dedicated to two important gods, it encloses two central sanctuaries approached by two separate axes across the enfilade of halls, which here number five instead of four.

The subsidiary buildings are in a ruinous state, but it is still possible to see the remains of a Birth House and a small temple dedicated to the goddess Hathor.

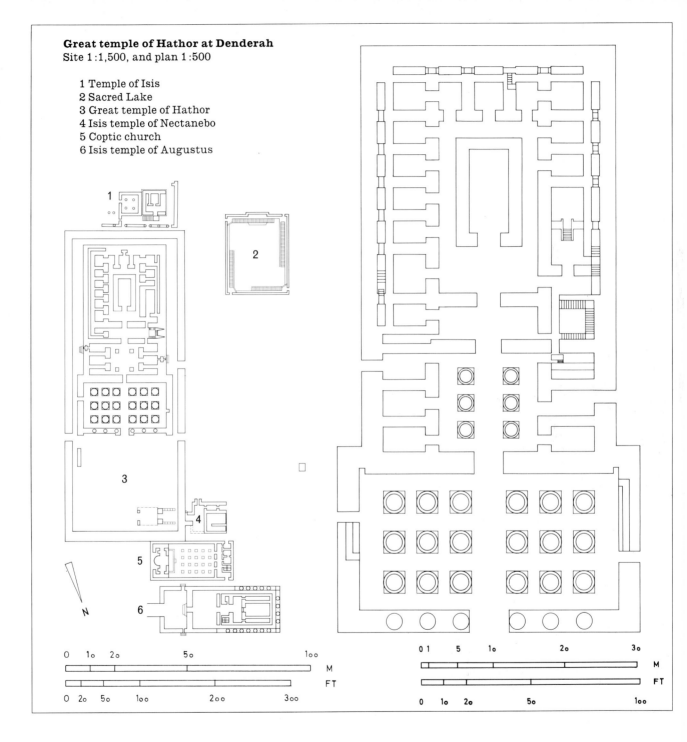

**Great temple of Hathor at Denderah**
Site 1:1,500, and plan 1:500

1 Temple of Isis
2 Sacred Lake
3 Great temple of Hathor
4 Isis temple of Nectanebo
5 Coptic church
6 Isis temple of Augustus

# Temple of Kom Ombo
Site 1 :3,000, plan 1 :750 and details of capitals 1 :150

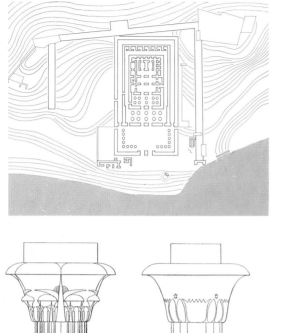

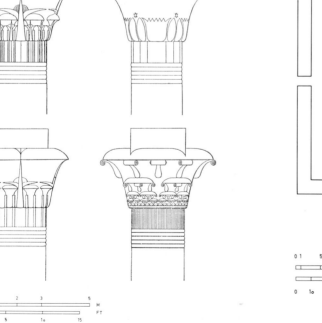

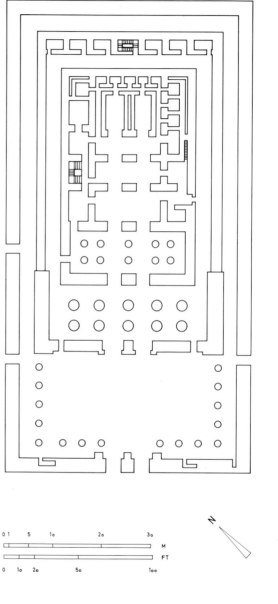

# 4. The Main Evolutionary Lines of Egyptian Architecture

The history of Egyptian architecture spreads over close on three thousand years; its development is based on religious, aesthetic and technical factors, using a formal vocabulary that changes little. The fundamentals of the permanent structure of Egyptian architecture are the reflection of the unchanging elements in the country's geography, society, culture and religion. We have seen, however, that individual art styles, particularly with regard to architecture, correspond to the successive historical stages summarized in Chapter I. The differences between these styles are as pronounced as those separating the various stages of other cultures, but they are particularly difficult to describe. That this is so is especially due to the scanty evidence left by certain periods and the highly incomplete nature of existing publications. The difficulty is also due to the nature of the changes which were very seldom caused by the use of new features. There are no changes similar to those marking the progress of Romanesque art to Gothic or Gothic to Classic and we seldom meet with those alterations in detail found in Gothic interiors which allow the accurate dating of a church from a section of molding, the decoration of a capital, or the design of a window tracery. The changes in Egyptian architecture are probably as profound, but more subtle and subjective; they lie in the choice made between a limited number of features, their frequency and interrelation, and in the general proportion of buildings, the arrangement of their decoration and the management of their lighting. Even unimportant modifications to one of these elements are enough to make a profound change in the character of the buildings and the atmosphere of their interiors. Unfortunately, the study of any one of these factors is exceedingly difficult with the documentation at our disposal. Let us take the case of lighting whose essential part in the definition of interior spaces has already been explained. The openings or windows are almost always in the upper parts of the buildings which have, of course, suffered most damage. When they are preserved, a few publications indicate their position, but seldom the direction they impart to the light and hardly ever the exact area illuminated which is, from our point of view, of primary importance. In the field of decoration the almost total disappearance of color places us at a disadvantage. The analysis of overall proportions is always one of the most difficult tasks to carry out: the basic objective criteria are the hardest to define and, for want of a large number of precise documents, they can only be assessed with the help of such vague terms as slender, compact or elongated, or too subjective ones, like stiff, austere, graceful, vigorous, and so on. The use of such adjectives is indispensable, but they should be supported by objective numerical data which we do not possess.

My purpose in these last few pages is to show that this development really exists and to point out its general tendencies with special reference to the most readily available factors: the modifications made in the choice of features, and of supports, in particular. In an architecture whose ceilings are almost invariably horizontal, whose wall surfaces are unbroken by windows and whose copings, at any rate after the Fifth Dynasty, always make use of a cornice with torus molding, supports are the most variable feature, not only from one period, but even from one temple to another. There is an even more banal reason for their importance: the place occupied by them in the interior space. The thickness and spacing of the columns, in other words the length of the architraves, were dictated to the architects by their experience of the resistance of the materials employed; this led them to highly approximate solutions which did not, in fact, greatly differ from those adopted by Greek architects and which might be selected by contemporary builders faced with similar problems. With a method of roofing as

weighty as slabs or horizontal architraves, it was hardly possible for them to make their pillars more slender or space them out further. In a hall containing more than ten pillars or columns, these prevent almost all the side views which could allow one to sum up the general proportions; the eye can follow only one aisle, or two at right angles, and the supports form the boundaries of the interior space for the spectator—in other words, the essential feature of the architecture.

## Old Kingdom

This book begins with the tomb complex of Zoser, the first monument in Egyptian, and possibly in world, history to be completely built of stone. The adoption of the new material and the development of the ideas behind it, the chief of which was probably the desire to create an enduring and more monumental architecture, were to result in basic modifications, but, in this first stage, they brought about little change in

Lower temple of the Bent Pyramid (Reconstruction by Ricke)

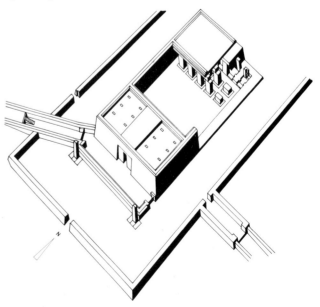

Façade of the lower temple of Chephren

style or form. Apart from the pyramid, Zoser's buildings are no more than earlier constructions of brick, mud, reeds and timber transposed into stone. Imhotep reproduced a light-weight architecture in stone, almost like theatre scenery designed to last for ever, with massive blocks, half-open blind doors and sham beams. The roofs were often arched because this strengthened the resistance of the timber or reed coverings; the walls were reinforced by fine, fluted pilasters set close against them; the interior spaces had no pillars or free-standing columns, only wall supports strengthened at each end by bundles of palm or tree trunks; the huge walls were given a rhythm by alternating projections and re-entrants causing an interplay of light and shade, and a great variety of forms were juxtaposed with one another. A hundred years later, first at Dahshur and then at Giza, we are faced with an entirely different type of architecture: instead of lively surfaces broken by pilasters, decorative friezes, projections and re-entrants and lightened by arched roofs and flutings, we find strictly flat, elongated surfaces broken only by a few rectangular doors. In place of the many differently-shaped buildings included in Zoser's vast complex are the two simple, similar masses of the upper and lower

temples linked by a descending approach. Inside, the geometrical severity of the smooth pillars is softened by the statues, the arrangement of different-colored stone, an economical use of carved decoration, and the interplay of light. There has been complete elimination of anything directly recalling the materials of the past. This represents a basic change of aesthetic which cannot be explained merely by a modified approach to the question of forms and their adaptation to a new material. As we have already seen, fundamental changes in theology and the royal cult must have intervened.

In order not to misunderstand the meaning of this development, we must realize that, as Ricke has so expertly pointed out, it really concerned only monumental religious architecture— royal tomb complexes and subsidiary private tombs. The knowledge that we have of secular architecture and minor religious buildings shows that in these spheres there was no abandonment of arched roofs, pilasters (as in the shelter of the great bark of Cheops discovered near his pyramid in 1954) or decorative motifs. Thus we are not dealing merely with a modification of taste but with a changed concept of architecture and the aims pursued by architects. Austerity and extremely simplified forms were sought after as a means of endowing the huge buildings with greater religious efficacy and increasing their monumentality. The use of stone guided this movement and made it easier but was probably not the determining factor. This trend towards ever more simplified forms is most clearly revealed in the lower temple of Chephren, the only one of the Old Kingdom sufficiently well preserved to give us a direct aesthetic impression of the whole complex. It must have marked the apogee of the movement which continued to exert its influence until the beginning of the Fifth Dynasty.

The tomb complex of Sahura, second king of the Fifth Dynasty, which has been very thoroughly restored, allows us to note another basic transformation of the monumental conception. This was first indicated by the adoption of much lighter floral columns instead of pillars: this alone was sufficient to transform completely the interior spaces of halls and courtyards which lost the geometrical stiffness imposed on them by bare rectangular surfaces. Simultaneously, copings with cornices and torus moldings made their appearance, making the massive exteriors rather less like blockhouses. The façades of

Lower temple of Sahura (Reconstruction by Borchardt)

the lower temple are open wide to the exterior, two vast porticoes with plant columns replacing the narrow rectangular openings of Chephren's temple. Finally, the halls scooped out within the monumental buildings tend to take up more space than the massive walls which lose their thickness. Thus the Fifth Dynasty adopted a monumental architecture that was less ambitious both in style and dimensions and more resembling secular architecture, from which it must have borrowed the floral columns. It was also less austere, lighter and more diverse, expressing its theological program in a more concrete manner by the adoption of purely symbolic features—floral columns probably assumed their symbolic role at this time—and by richer carved representational decoration. This style lasted throughout the Fifth and probably the Sixth Dynasties. It must, however, be noted that the complex of Pepy II, which has a strictly classical arrangement of halls, includes a return

Courtyard of the upper temple of Sahura (Reconstruction by Borchardt)

to square pillars and a lower temple with one simple rectangular door, thus possibly marking a limited reversion to the traditions of the Fourth Dynasty. This theory cannot, however, be confirmed as the temples of his predecessors and successors are still buried in the sand.

## Middle Kingdom

The greatest gap in our knowledge of Egyptian art concerns the architecture of the Middle Kingdom. The pyramids of the period have been reduced to shapeless heaps and their original dimensions cannot always be determined. Very little is left, too, of the temples which stood near them. The main outlines of the pyramid-temple of Mentuhotep have been restored, but this is, in many ways, such an exceptional monument that its use to define the style of the period is highly questionable. The mastaba tombs surrounding the pyramids are also in a very ruinous state. The only examples that can be considered seriously are two small buildings: the pavilion of Sesostris I at Karnak

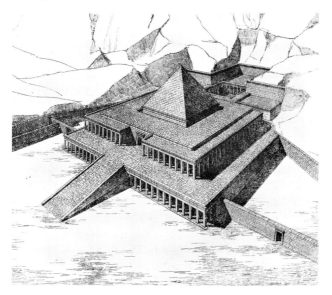

Tomb complex of Mentuhotep (Reconstruction by Curelly)

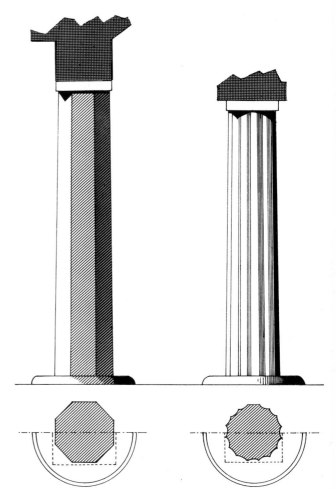

Polygonal columns of the Middle Kingdom

and the chapel at Medinet Madi built by Amenemhat III, the first dating from the beginning, the second from the end, of the Middle Kingdom. It is also possible to make use of the principal rock tombs of the provincial governors at Aswan and Beni Hasan and secondary ones at Bersheh, Meir, Qaw el Kebir and elsewhere. Historical factors such as the progressive rise of the provincial nobility probably explain the fact that almost all these tombs date from the first half of the Old Kingdom. Thus we find ourselves in a highly difficult situation: if we wish to compare the architecture of the Middle Kingdom with that of the Old Kingdom we can only do so with buildings that differ completely in type, size and function—large temples and a small pavilion—which is risky. In this case we should forego the comparison of groups of buildings and limit ourselves to individual features.

To the best of our knowledge, the architecture of the early Middle Kingdom is distinguished by a taste for geometrical, non-representational features such as the square pillars of the pavilion of Sesostris I, the temple of Mentuhotep and the tombs at Aswan, and the polygonal columns with eight or sixteen faces again at the temple of Mentuhotep, and at Beni Hasan. No floral columns have been found in the temples and few in the tombs, but reliefs and models show that they must have been frequently used in secular architecture. In the return to abstraction there is a reversion to the traditions of the Fourth Dynasty, but some of the legacy of the Fifth is still preserved in the lightening of

Entrance portico to a Middle Kingdom tomb at Beni Hasan

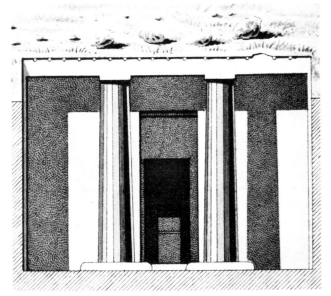

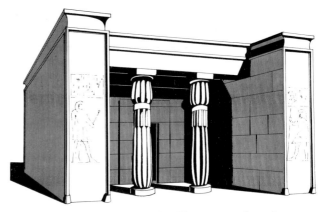

Chapel at Medinet Madi (Reconstruction by Naumann)

the exteriors by the use of copings with cornices and frontal porticoes, and of the interiors by the use of polygonal columns which are much slimmer than those of the Fourth Dynasty, and the reduced thickness of the walls.

If we seek to compare the architecture of the first and second halves of the Middle Kingdom, we are provided with two buildings of similar size but quite different technical levels, and designed for different purposes. Moreover, the conclusions drawn from this comparison cannot be substantiated as the chapel of Amenemhat III is almost the sole surviving building of the late Twelfth Dynasty. The most striking feature of this small temple at Medinet Madi is the theoretical reappearance of floral columns resembling bunches of papyrus. That their presence in a building of this period, along with their absence in the most important ones preceding it, is not merely due to the chance of preservation seems to be confirmed by the high proportion of columns of this type among the scanty remains of contemporary monuments and those of slightly later date, particularly at Bubastis and Medamud. This is almost the only finding that the architectural monuments allow us to make and it is not easy to interpret this isolated phenomenon. In this case, it is very tempting to have recourse to other branches of art where there is not the same scarcity of survivals and it is possible to gain a fairly clear and coherent idea of their evolution. We must, however, remember that when we have separate knowledge of the development of two arts over the same period of time, it is highly tempting to stress the parallels between them, pointing out their indisputable characteristics and appearing to reconstruct one by means of the other. This kind of exercise, properly carried out, is one of the fundamentals of art history, but, for our purpose, its rules are too obscure and it seems preferable merely to make statements. Nevertheless, it is tempting to see in these two papyrus columns evidence of a partial abandonment of the tendency to geometrical abstraction in vogue at the beginning of the dynasty in favor of a more expressionist, realistic, lyrical type of art.

## New Kingdom

The architecture of the Eighteenth Dynasty developed from that of the Middle Kingdom but, if our deductions from the few remains of the late Twelfth Dynasty are correct, it was the art of the early Middle Kingdom that the Tuthmoses and Amenhoteps wished to imitate. This return to ancient sources was not limited to architecture. It is also evident in the spheres of relief sculpture and painting. All the features used by architects in the first half of the Eighteenth Dynasty are ones which already played a dominant part in the architecture of the early New Kingdom. Sufficient proof of this may be gained by an analysis of the temple of Hatshepsut at Deir el Bahari and a comparison of it with the neighboring temple of Mentuhotep. Here it is no longer a question of common tendencies but a matter of obvious inspiration bordering on direct imitation. From the earlier temple Senmut took his long porticoes with square pillars rising in terraces, the wide ascending ramp and the inner sanctuary embed-

ded in the mountain; it is also possible that he borrowed the idea of the strict harmony of the building with the landscape. The range of Osiride pillars forming the third level of the temple is not found in Mentuhotep's, nor are the similar features placed beneath the trees at the sides of the approach, but they may possibly have been borrowed from buildings of the time of Sesostris I: there are several pillars of this type from Lisht and Karnak which reproduce this king's features. The entrance colonnade to the sanctuary of Anubis and the north portico with their sixteen-sided columns are extended versions of the façades of some of the tombs at Beni Hasan. The sistrum columns in the sanctuary of Hathor also have their Middle Kingdom prototypes, though dating from the end of the period. Senmut's originality and genius are revealed in the proportions and detail of the plan and the way in which the temple blends with its setting.

Most of the other monuments of the Eighteenth Dynasty employed the same features. Sometimes, however, we find examples of papyrus columns very similar in form and proportion to those of Medinet Madi; those in front of the small sanctuary in the first court at Luxor are attributed by some to the Middle Kingdom and by others to the reigns of Hatshepsut or Tuthmosis III in the Eighteenth Dynasty. It is possible that they may have been executed by Senmut as he is known to have worked at Luxor.

It is easy enough to tabulate the points these two periods of architecture have in common, but far more difficult to explain the differences between them. For this purpose it is once more necessary to compare buildings of different function and dimensions and to resort to far more subjective criteria such as proportions, lightness, severity and atmosphere. That a great difference must have existed in the character of the architecture of these two periods is made almost certain by those which may be noted in other branches of art, despite the outward resemblances caused by a conscious desire to return to the disciplines of the past after the decadence of the Second Intermediary Period: forms are, for the most part, lighter, softer, more disguised, there is less severe, geometrical stylization, and proportions are more slender. More obvious care is taken over the decoration and the aesthetic side, resulting in an art of greater refinement and delicacy, almost feminine in type. Such vague qualifications, which may be legitimately applied to some of the sculptures, must suffice to give some idea of where to look for differences. The attempt to achieve a greater effect of lightness may be noted in the more frequent use of polygonal columns of sixteen sides or more, especially in interior spaces. At Deir el Bahari, the lower portico offers a strange individual feature: the outer supports are semi-polygonal, that is to say from the courtyard they appear as square pillars, but from within the portico as sixteen-sided columns. The inner range, on the other hand, is made up of ordinary sixteen-sided columns. It is tempting to suppose that Senmut wished to present a flat, stiff façade, unbroken by any rounded form and, at the same time, to lighten the interior of his narrow portico.

Of all the stylistic changes that took place in the history of Egyptian architecture, that between the Eighteenth and Nineteenth Dynasties is the one that can best be observed owing to the relatively high number of examples surviving from both periods, similar in dimensions, function and technical level, and also on account of the clarity of the transformations. The buildings of the immediate successors of Hatshepsut and Tuthmosis III are few, but their scanty remains are sufficient to preclude the idea that basic modifications took place during the reigns of Amenhotep II and Tuthmosis IV. The turning point was during the reign of Amenhotep III, and the pace probably quickened during the Amarnian Period to result, under Ramesses II, in the classic formal system that was to endure throughout the Ramesside Period. We have already noted the tendency to the colossal in royal statues and commemorative or funerary temples that was a common feature of the buildings of Amenhotep III and Ramesses II and probably accompanied important changes in the royal theology. Once more, it is in the choice of supports that the most obvious, most clearly effective changes can be found. Geometrical features gradually yield to columns with plant motifs and Osiride pillars which completely transform the atmosphere of the temple interiors. These plant columns also change their shape. The type most often used throughout the New Kingdom represents a number of stalks carrying flowers in bud which are often known as papyrus columns with closed capitals, though the Egyptians sometimes called them lotus.

In the Eighteenth Dynasty, as in the Middle Kingdom, the stalks were carved in high relief along the shafts; these are known as papyrus-bundle columns. There are usually eight stalks, each of which has its center stressed by a sharp vertical ridge representing the shape of the papyrus plant whose section is almost triangular. There is a strongly defined narrowing at the foot of the column and at the base of the capital. These features give the column a keen clarity of line which lightens its general silhouette. In the reign of Amenhotep III, especially at Luxor, the center ridge is hardly marked, sometimes not at all, and the channels separating the stalks are less deep; in these cases, the general effect is more massive, more regular and softer, although the proportions are similar. This tendency showed a pronounced increase in the Amarnian Period, while the proportions became even heavier. In the reign of Sety I columns with slim shafts appeared beside fairly heavy papyrus-bundle columns. They retain the outline of

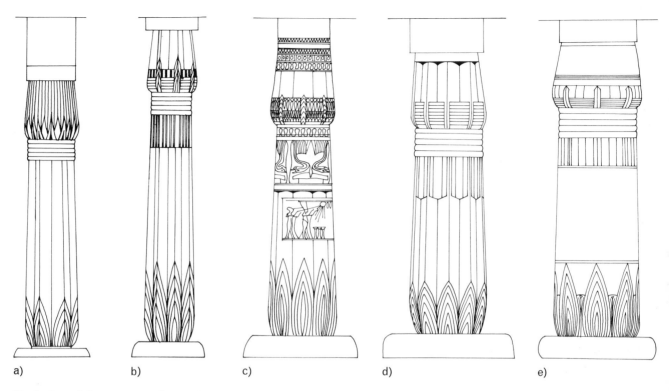

a)       b)       c)       d)       e)

Evolution of the papyrus column with closed capital
(a) Fifth Dynasty; (b) Eighteenth Dynasty, reign of Tuthmosis III;

(c) Reign of Amenhotep IV; (d) Nineteenth Dynasty, reign of Sety I; (e) Twentieth Dynasty, reign of Ramesses III

the bunch of flowers, the compression at the base and the gradual narrowing towards the capital, but, at every level the section is circular and the few details which are preserved are only indicated in very low relief. It was this type of column which was predominant to the end of the Ramesside Period. The reign of Amenhotep III also saw the introduction of the bell-shaped column into monumental religious architecture: these are sometimes known as papyrus columns with open capitals and represent a single stalk supporting a flower in bloom. Under the Ramessides, this type of support usually bordered the center aisle of the great hypostyle halls. Polygonal columns almost completely disappeared and square pillars were used only very occasionally. A complete alteration in the interiors of the great halls and courtyards of the temples resulted from this change of supports. Within the halls, the shafts of the columns conceal the walls and themselves form the boundaries of the interior space; all straight lines and flat surfaces have disappeared and the eye is merely caught by a number of curves outlining heavy, swollen masses, their plant-like character stressed by their decoration. There is a change, too, in the ornamentation. Instead of the plain, vertical lines that ran down the faces of the columns of the Eighteenth Dynasty, standing out from the whiteness of the rest of the shaft, a host of multi-colored scenes, divinities and plant details covered the supports, increasing the impression of abundance and heavy profusion produced by the architecture.

This decoration is by no means inferior to that of the Eighteenth Dynasty. In the ornamentation of the large surfaces of pylons and exterior walls, it gives proof of a freedom and breadth of composition capable of organizing full-scale scenes without splitting them up into separate registers and, at the same time, of preserving their traditional clarity, at any rate as long as the colors survived to make the design stand out. It was also richer and more highly colored. This type of art has often been called Baroque and this it undoubtedly is in its taste for overloading and curved lines; where this does not apply is in the extent to which it marks a drift away from abstraction to a more direct form of expression and a greater use of natural forms. We should not expect terms created to define a period of Western art to be exactly applicable to such a different art form; the comparison, however, if taken in a very wide sense, is not too far from the mark in this case.

## Late Period

The tendency towards ever heavier masses and more solid proportions which marked architecture at any rate up to the reign of Ramesses III, does not seem to have continued after the Twentieth Dynasty. In the troubled times that followed, the political and economic situation prevented the conception or, at least, the execution of great architectural projects. Nevertheless, many small chapels and annexes to earlier temples were built. It is possible to note in these, as in other branches of art, a return to the traditions of the Eighteenth Dynasty and the Middle Kingdom, and a revival in technical interest, the origin of which it is difficult to determine. During the Twenty-sixth Dynasty political and economic revival allowed the execution of ambitious building programs, but the chief efforts were confined to the Delta where the kings had fixed their capital and the increase of trade with the Mediterranean world encouraged wealth and activity. In this part of the country conditions were less favorable to the preservation of monuments so that this dynasty remains one of those which are more poorly represented. From the period of Persian domination which followed there survive the partial remains of a temple in the Khargeh Oasis which, in its layout and especially its decoration, heralds some of the features of the late temples. It is, however, in the Thirtieth Dynasty (although unfortunately only in minor buildings) that it is possible to distinguish the chief transformations which were to typify the art of the Graeco-Roman Period. In every branch of art there is great continuity between what was executed in the years both before and after the arrival of Alexander in Egypt. The installation of the Macedonian kings and their administration marked no aesthetic break.

It is not possible to know what a complete temple of the Thirtieth Dynasty looked like, but, in the surviving buildings of the period, we may note the first appearance of a type of column called composite which was to remain the most distinctive characteristic of the last Egyptian temples. From this period, too, date the earliest examples of the stone shrines which were to be standard features of the main sanctuaries. Birth Houses are also found, and the great monumental gateways which break the brick enclosing wall in front of the pylons—for which reason they are sometimes known as pro-pylons—come into being and assume their definitive shape. Moreover, building technique already resembles that of the Graeco-Roman Period, so much so that the first pylon at Karnak, whose masonry is considered by some as typically Ptolemaic owing to the uniformity and slightly reduced size of the blocks and the increased care taken over the construction of the core, is attributed by others to one of the Nectanebos.

It is quite possible that some of these changes

took place earlier—those relating to technique had been in the offing since the Twenty-fifth Dynasty—and it is highly unlikely that the type of late temple found at Edfu, Denderah, or Kom Ombo was entirely fixed in every detail. The development must have continued during the reigns of the first two Ptolemies after which there were few changes in the formula until the end of Pharaonic civilization. The great hall at Esna, conceived in the second century A.D., differs very little from the one at Edfu dating from the second century B.C. Monumental religious architecture of the Graeco-Roman Period was not inferior to that of earlier epochs but, after a period of invention and renewal which included the Thirtieth Dynasty and the beginning of Greek domination, it became static. This fidelity to tradition enabled it to avoid the decadence noticeable in contemporary reliefs and sculptures.

It is possible to identify a late building at a glance from the presence of composite columns or capitals. The columns are almost always shaped like the old bell-shaped ones—papyrus columns with open capitals—but on the capitals, often in high relief and with very little attempt at stylization, are depicted a variety of plants, intertwined and one above the other. The shafts are almost always more or less cylindrical, narrowing slightly towards the top, and the curved lines so prominent in the Ramesside Period have disappeared. The polygonal pillars and columns so much favored in the Eighteenth Dynasty, and Osiride pillars, are no longer used. Variety is probably the chief new characteristic introduced by these capitals. In the porticoes of the courtyards and within the great halls each column has its equivalent column symmetrically placed on the other side of the axis, but almost every capital on the same side is different, either in its arrangement or in its choice of plants. This variety linked to the contrast between the simple, geometrical form of the shaft and the rich, naturalistic decoration of the capital gives the latter an importance which it never possessed in earlier buildings. So far as the lighting allows, they immediately attract and hold the eye. These columns are clearly not the only contribution of late architecture, but they are the most readily identifiable. The arrangement of the decoration is changed: the large scenes of the Ramesside temples are replaced by a similar succession of offerings set out in narrow, horizontal registers of equal area. In each of these almost the entire surface unoccupied by the pictures is filled with texts yielding the utmost pleasure to philologists and historians of religion. The interior lighting probably achieved a maximum degree of subtlety and mystery. The fairly uniform distribution of light in the great halls of the Ramesside Period by means of windows set above the central aisles was abandoned in favor of a system of slender beams directed towards selected points as in the Old Kingdom, but probably devised with more varied ingenuity.

None of these new features can be attributed to direct Hellenistic influence which, if it played any part at all, must have been quite unconscious and is difficult to detect. Some think it may be found in the more forceful modeling of sculptural decoration and the greater care devoted to constructional technique. Theoretically, temple architecture remained completely impervious to it at a time when many other hybrid forms of art were developing. These included sculptures of kings or private individuals in which Greek-style draperies covered figures in the standard Egyptian poses, the architecture of tombs including some at Hermopolis, funerary reliefs, and sarcophagi and paintings. The explanation for this contrast has been outlined in Chapter I: the art both of the court and that of private individuals was created either for the wealthiest Egyptians who were connected with the king or the central administration, or for the Greek middle class which succumbed to certain aspects of Egyptian religion. The temples erected in the names of the Greek or Roman monarchs were built by and for the priesthood, to which the architects belonged and which lived apart from the Greek world.

The temples became the sole surviving centers of the ancient culture which the priests jealously defended against foreign interference. In the field of ideas and philosophy, they could not remain insensible to the strong intellectual currents that flooded the Mediterranean world, but, where architecture was concerned, they succeeded in achieving almost complete isolation. This resistance of monumental architecture to foreign influences was, in fact, by no means new to Egypt. In the Middle and especially the New Kingdoms, the influence of Syrian art was particularly clear in certain spheres such as the military works of the Ramesside Period of which the fortified tower of Medinet Habu serves as an example: these were practically copied from Syrian prototypes. In the decorative arts and domestic architecture may be found an abundance of motifs imported from Crete and the Near East, but these were not introduced into the patrician arts of sculpture and religious architecture. Here we find the same difference between a decorative and monumental aesthetic which we have already encountered when dealing with the style of the Old Kingdom.

Thus, the evolution of Egyptian architecture does not present itself as a continuous movement accompanied by the progressive insertion of new elements which eliminate the old ones, but as a balanced choice of features all of which exist side by side, at least in secular architecture, and some of which correspond better than others to the individual needs of monumental expression at different periods. It is strange to note, on perhaps three occasions—during the passage of the Fourth to the Fifth Dynasty, probably between the early and late Twelfth Dynasty and, finally, between the Eighteenth and Nineteenth Dynasties—the replacement of an art that tended to be geometrical by one which expressed its symbols with the help of more immediate representational features.

## Conclusion

My purpose in this text has not been to formulate the results obtained by the architects, but the way in which they were attained and the state of mind which produced them. There has been little mention of the temples as works of art, except in the last chapter. They have not been described, compared, or placed beside monuments erected by other civilizations. In other words, this has not been a history of architecture, but an introduction to it, a summary of facts which can throw light on it, but which cannot be deduced from photographs or observation of the actual buildings.

The real Egyptian forms must be discovered from the illustrations. These are so devised that the reader may feel, as he turns the pages, that he is walking slowly through the ruins, letting his eye linger over details such as capitals, carvings or points of technique. A monument is made up of the sum of all these aspects and a single view can give only a false impression. The adoption of this method has restricted the illustrations to a small number of buildings and has resulted in many other buildings, perhaps just as fine, being passed over.

Some of the best known have been omitted as good photographs of them may be found elsewhere; for this reason there are no reproductions of Luxor and hardly any of Karnak. Other buildings equally meriting a place here include the temple of Sety I at Gurna and the island sanctuaries of Philae, but to have given space to illustrating them would have meant a less complete picture of those that have been chosen.

# Chronological Table

| Dates C. | Principal Monuments illustrated or named | Main Stages of Egyptian History |
|---|---|---|
| 3100 | | End of Prehistoric Period, invention of writing, unification of country |
| | Great brick tombs of Saqqara | Thinite Period: Dynasties I and II |
| 2700-2650 | Funerary complex of Zoser | **Old Kingdom**<br>Dynasty III |
| 2650-2500 | Pyramids of Sneferu, Cheops, Chephren and Mycerinus | Dynasty IV: statues of Chephren (Cairo), Rahotep and Nefret (Cairo) |
| 2500-2350 | Pyramid of Sahura; sun temple of Ne-user-ra; mastaba Ptahhotep; pyramid of Unas | Dynasty V: statue of seated scribe (Paris)<br>Book of proverbs of Ptahhotep |
| 2350-2200 | Mastaba of Mereruka; pyramid of Pepy II | Dynasty VI |
| 2200-2050 | | **First Intermediate Period**<br>"Dialogue between a man and his soul" |
| 2050-2000 | Funerary temple of Mentuhotep | **Middle Kingdom**<br>Dynasty XI |
| 2000-1800 | Pavilion of Sesostris I at Karnak; tomb of Prince Sarenput at Aswan; fortress of Buhen; Chapel at Medinet Madi | Dynasty XII: statues of Sesostris III (Paris, Cairo, London); Ballad of Sinuhe |
| 1800-1580 | | **Second Intermediate Period**<br>Invasion of the Hyksos |
| 1580-1320 | Pavilion of Amenhotep I at Karnak; Obelisks of Tuthmosis I and Hatshepsut at Karnak; Temple of Hatshepsut at Deir el Bahari | **New Kingdom:**<br>Dynasty XVIII |
| 1484-1450 | Temple of Luxor | Reign of Tuthmosis III<br>Amenhotep IV (or Akhenaten) and Nefretete; religious revolution of Amarna; reign of Tut-ankh-amon |
| 1320-1200<br>1304-1238<br>1200-1085 | Temple of Sety I at Abydos<br>Ramesseum and temples of Abu Simbel<br>Temple of Medinet Habu<br>Tombs of Ramesses VI and Ramesses IX | Dynasty XIX<br>Reign of Ramesses II<br>Dynasty XX: reign of Ramesses III |
| 1085-950<br>950-730<br>751-656 | | Dynasty XXI: period of priest-kings<br>Dynasty XXII: Libyan period<br>Dynasty XXV: Ethiopian domination |

| Historical Landmarks | Dates C. |
|---|---|
| | 3100 |
| | 2700-2650 |
| First Sumerian Period (c.2800-2370)<br>Formation of First Empire of Akkad by Sargon | 2650-2500 |
| | 2500-2350 |
| | 2350-2200 |
| Neo-Sumerian Period (c.2230-2000)<br>Gudea, Prince of Lagash, third dynasty of Ur | 2200-2050 |
| | 2050-2000 |
| First dynasty of Babylon: Hammurabi (c. 1789-1747); Crete: Middle Minoan | 2000-1800 |
| Beginning of Mycenaean Period | 1800-1580 |
| Late Minoan<br>Rise of Hittie Empire | 1580-1320 |
| Collaps of power of Crete | 1484-1450 |
| | 1320-1200 |
| Siege of Troy | 1304-1238 |
| "Peoples of the sea" overthrow Hittie Empire and ravage Syria | 1200-1085 |
| David, King of Israel | 1085-950 |
| Solomon, King of Israel | 950-730 |
| The Assyrian Empire of height of its power | 751-656 |

| Dates C. | Principal Monuments illustrated or named | Main Stages of Egyptian History |
|---|---|---|
| 664-525 | | Dynasty **XXVI**: Saite Renaissance, reign of Psamtik |
| 525-404 | | Dynasty **XXVII**: Egypt a province of the Persian Empire |
| 404-341 | | Dynasties **XXVIII-XXX**: last of the native dynasties, reign of Nectanebo II |
| 333 | | Conquest of Egypt by Alexander |
| 333-30 B.C. | Temple of Edfu (237-57 B.C.), Temples of Denderah (c.80 B.C.-50 A.D.), Kom Ombo (c.180 B.C.-30 A.D.) and Esna (c.96-161 A.D.) | **Ptolemaic Period** The country is governed by Macedonian rulers<br><br>**Roman Period** Egypt a Roman province |

| Historical Landmarks | Dates c. |
|---|---|
| Fall of Assyrian Empire; Nebuchadnezzar conquers Jerusalem<br>Cyrus founds Persian Empire | 664-525 |
| Persian wars; Periclean Athens<br>Beginnings of Roman history | 525-404 |
| Plato, Praxiteles, Demosthenes<br>Philip of Macedon | 404-341 |
| Conquest of Alexander the Great | 333 |
| Strife between the descendants of Alexander's generals who partitioned his empire | 333-30 B.C. |

# Bibliography

## I. Architecture

There is no book that deals with Egyptian architecture in its entirety. Apart from those devoted to the history of art which include architecture to some extent, it is necessary to have recourse to monographs dealing with a single aspect or period.

Badawy, I.
A History of Egyptian Architecture, Vol. I: From the earliest times to the end of the Old Kingdom, Giza (Egypt), 1954.

Clarke, Somers and R. Engelbach
Ancient Egyptian Masonry. Oxford, University Press, 1930.

Edwards, I. E. S.
Pyramids of Egypt. London, Max Parrish, 1961

Jéquier, G.
Manuel d'Archéologie égyptienne. Paris, Picard, 1924

Jéquier, G.
L'architecture et la décoration dans l'ancienne Egypte (photographic documentation only): 1. Les temples memphites et thébains des origines à la XVIIIe dynastie. Paris, 1920. 2. Les temples ramessides et saïtes de la XIXe à la XXXe dynastie, Paris, 1922. 3. Les temples ptolémaïques et romains. Paris, 1924

Lauer, J.-P.
Le problème des pyramides. Paris, Payot, 1948

Lauer, J.-P.
Histoire monumentale des pyramides d'Egypte. Cairo, Institut français, 1962, T. I: Les pyramides à degrés

Ricke, H.
Beiträge zur ägyptischen Bauforschung und Altertums-kunde, Fasc. 4: Bemerkungen zur ägyptischen Baukunst des Alten Reiches. Zurich, 1944. (Work for specialists; heavy reading, but vital for an understanding of Egyptian architecture.)

Vandier, J.
Manuel d'Archéologie égyptienne. Paris, Picard, T. I, Les époques de formation, Vol. 2: Les trois premières dynasties, 1952.—T. II, Les grandes époques, Vol. 1: L'architecture funéraire, 1954; Vol. 2: L'architecture religieuse et civile, 1955

## II. History and civilization

Drioton, E. and Vandier, J.
L'Egypte. Clio, Paris, Presses Universitaires de France, Fourth edition, 1963

Helck-Otto
Kleines Wörterbuch der Ägyptologie. Wiesbaden, O. Harrassowitz, 1956

Kees, H.
Kulturgeschichte des alten Orients. Munich, C. Beck, 1933

Posener, G., Sauneron, S. and Yoyotte, J.
Dictionnaire de la civilisation égyptienne. Paris, Hazan, 1959

## III. Religion

Bonnet, H.
Reallexikon der ägyptischen Religionsgeschichte. Berlin, W. de Gruyter, 1952

Cerny, J.
Ancient Egyptian Religion. London, Hutchinson's University Library, 1952

Morenz, S.
Ägyptische Religion. Stuttgart, W. Kohlhammer. (French translation: La religion égyptienne. Paris, Payot, 1962)

Sauneron, S.
Les prêtres dans l'ancienne Egypte. Paris, Ed. du Seuil, 1957

## IV. Literature

Erman, A.
Die Literatur der Ägypter. Leipzig, 1923. (English translation by A. M. Blackmann. London, 1927)

Lefebvre, G.
Romans et contes égyptiens. Paris, Maisonneuve, 1949

Schott, S.
Altägyptische Liebeslieder. Zurich, Artemis, 1950. (Translated into French by P. Krieger. Paris, Maisonneuve, 1956)

## V. Art

Aldred, C.
1. Old Kingdom Art in Ancient Egypt, 1949
2. Middle Kingdom Art in Ancient Egypt, 1950
3. New Kingdom Art in Ancient Egypt, 1951. London, Tiranti

Lange, K. and Hirmer, M.
Ägypten. Munich, Hirmer. (English translation: Egypt. London, Phaidon Press, 1956)

Smith, W. S.
The Art and Architecture of Ancient Egypt. Penguin Books, Pelican History of Art, 1958

Vandier, J.
Manuel d'archéologie égyptienne, T. III: La statuaire. Paris, Picard, 1958

# Acknowledgements

It has not been possible to expand the text of this book with notes, so I have been unable to record my sources and debts of gratitude in the course of the work. Some of the former may be found in the short bibliography. I have relied especially on the writings of Clarke and Engelbach, Ricke, Lauer and Vandier, but I have also made use of many specialist articles that do not figure in the bibliography, particularly by Lauer, Daumas, de Wit, Edgerton, Yoyette and Sauneron. Specialists will easily identify my borrowings. There are others, too, made from unpublished sources which I should specially mention here: I have frequently made use of notes taken during Barguet's lectures at the École des Hautes Études. Also, some of the theories advanced in the text, particularly those regarding the connection of aesthetics with architecture, have been stimulated or modified in the course of conversations with J. Yoyette and Sauneron, who have provided me with some unpublished texts.

When I have quoted ancient texts, I have often used the translations of other Egyptologists and must make special acknowledgement to Schott for the 'Dialogue of a man with his soul'.

The photographer is particularly grateful to the Egyptian authorities for their assistance to him in his work. Special thanks are due to the Minister of Tourism and the U.A.R. Tourist Offices at Cairo and Geneva, the staff of the Egyptian Museum and those in charge of excavations, United Arab Airlines, and the U.A.R. Air Force which placed a military helicopter at his disposal to take photographs over Giza and Dahshur.

The archaeological work in progress at the Aswan tombs and the sites of Abu Simbel and Buhen are the subjects of three photographs from the sources credited below:
p.74 (Aswan) by courtesy of M. Georg Gerster (Zurich),
p.75 (Buhen) by courtesy of the Marburg Institute,
p.117 (Abu Simbel) by courtesy of UNESCO (Paris).